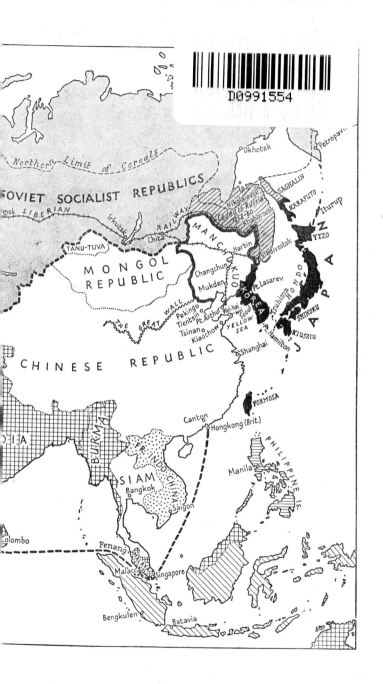

Northern Limit of Cereals

SOVIET SOCIALIST REPUBLICS

msk SIBERIAN

Okhotsk

Petropav

Nikolaievsk
Ceded to Russia
1858-60
Khabarovsk

SAGHALIN

KARAFUTO

Iturup

Irkutsk

RAILWAY

Chita

TANU-TUVA

MONGOL
REPUBLIC

MANCHUKUO

Harbin

Vladivostok

YEZO

Changchun

Mukden

HONDO

KOREA

Pt.Lasarev

THE GREAT WALL

Pekingo
Tientsin
Tsinano
Kiaochow

Pt.Arthur
Wei-hai
Wei
Seoul

YELLOW
SEA

Tsushima

Hamilton

SHIKOKU

KIUSHIU

JAPAN

CHINESE REPUBLIC

Shanghai

Canton

FORMOSA

Hongkong (Brit.)

DIA

BURMA

FR INDO-CHINA

SIAM

Bangkok

Saigon

PHILIPPINE Is.

Manila

Colombo

Penang

Malacca

Singapore

Bengkulen

Batavia

THE FAR EAST
IN
WORLD POLITICS

MARSHAL CHIANG KAI-SHEK

THE FAR EAST
IN
WORLD POLITICS

A STUDY IN
RECENT HISTORY

BY

G. F. HUDSON
Fellow of All Souls College

SECOND EDITION

OXFORD UNIVERSITY PRESS
LONDON : HUMPHREY MILFORD

OXFORD UNIVERSITY PRESS
AMEN HOUSE, E.C. 4
London Edinburgh Glasgow New York
Toronto Melbourne Capetown Bombay
Calcutta Madras
HUMPHREY MILFORD
PUBLISHER TO THE UNIVERSITY

First edition February 1937
Reprinted July 1937

Second edition April 1939, reprinted photographically in
Great Britain by LOWE & BRYDONE, PRINTERS, LTD.,
LONDON, from sheets of the first edition

Reprinted 1945

PREFACE

THIS book is an attempt to provide a short historical introduction to the present international situation in the Far East. The object has been to trace the policies of the principal Powers of the Far East in their relations with one another since the 'opening of the gates' of China and Japan by Western insistence less than a hundred years ago. The domestic affairs of the countries concerned have been left out of the picture except in so far as they have seemed to have some direct bearing on international relations. Such an exception has been made with regard to the difference between the Chinese and Japanese responses to the pressure of the Western nations in the nineteenth century, for no adequate comprehension of recent Far Eastern history is possible without an understanding of the factors which have given Japan the advantage over China in facility of adaptation to Western-made conditions.

The Far East is a region of the world which is most clearly demarcated in relation to the seaway round to the south of the Eurasian double continent. The Mediterranean, the Indian Ocean, and the Pacific are the three stages of this voyage, with Suez and Singapore as the points of division. The sharp turn round the corner at Singapore is the beginning of the Far East, which means Saigon, Hong Kong, Shanghai, and Kobe for ordinary shipping lines, and anything beyond up to the Bering Strait if the traveller can find a boat for it. The Far East is in fact the Pacific coastline of Asia with its hinterland and adjacent islands. For Europeans it is the other side of Asia; it can be reached by a ship going round Asia or by a railway across Asia. For Americans, on the other hand, especially if they live west of the Rockies, the Far East is the other side of the Pacific Ocean, to be reached by sailing straight across it, and it is not *eastern* at all, except by conventional usage. These angles of view correspond to the three historical lines of approach of the 'Western' nations to the region of the world with which we are dealing— through the Indian Ocean (Portuguese, Dutch, English, French), across northern Asia (Russians), and across the Pacific from North America (Spanish, U.S. Americans). They correspond also to the geographical axes of the three non-indigenous sovereignties which rank to-day as Great Powers in the Far East: England with her imperial chain, Gibraltar— Malta — Egypt — Aden — India — Malaya — Hong Kong, Russia with her one-piece territory from the Baltic to the Pacific, and the United States with her all-American Trans-Pacific airway, Hawaii—Midway—Wake—Guam—Manila.

Several Western Powers by reason of their territorial possessions and bases in the Far East play a part in its affairs such as no indigenous Far Eastern nation can play in Europe or the Americas. But Far Eastern politics are not simply colonial; we have here no sub-continent of 'natives' who are all the passive,

helpless subjects of arrangements or disputes between
'white men's' governments. Just before the Russo-
Japanese war General Dragomirov declared that 'Far
Eastern affairs are decided in Europe'. Since 1905
Europeans have been less inclined to make such asser-
tions. Japan has become a Great Power—one of the
seven states to which that title is generally allowed—
and when we speak of 'the situation in the Far East'
the most prominent theme of the mental picture is
no longer the rivalry of England, France, Germany,
and Russia, as it would have been in 1898, but Japan's
imperial expansion. To-day it is Japan, to-morrow it
may be China. In any case it is likely that in the
coming decades, through whatever agency of power,
the six hundred millions of human population concentrated in the Pacific islands and watershed area
from Java to Kamchatka will play a part in world
politics not incommensurate with their numerical
aggregation—between a quarter and a third of the
human race. Prophecy is no part of the business of
this book, but an effort has been made to provide a
summary of a century of regional history which may
be of some use for an understanding of current events.

For this new edition I have rewritten in part, and
largely added to, the final chapter in order to include some account of the present Sino-Japanese
war. The general scheme of the book remains un-
changed.   G. F. H.

OXFORD   *January* 1939

ERRATUM

Page 142, line 19, *for* Heitoukai
read Heikowtai

CONTENTS

I.	'THE FURTHER DEVELOPMENT OF THE EASTERN TRADE'	I
II.	THE OPENING OF THE GATES	I2
III.	THE WESTERNIZERS	27
IV.	THE EUROPEAN EMPIRES	50
V.	THE RAILWAY ACROSS ASIA	7I
VI.	THE BATTLE OF THE CONCESSIONS	9I
VII.	THE ANGLO-JAPANESE ALLIANCE	III
VIII.	THE REPULSE OF RUSSIA	I28
IX.	THE EVICTION OF GERMANY	I52
X.	THE WASHINGTON TREATIES	I83
XI.	THE MARCH OF THE KUOMINTANG	205
XII.	MANCHUKUO	234
XIII.	CONCLUSION	248
	INDEX	277

LIST OF PLATES

Marshal Chiang Kai-shek. By courtesy of the Chinese
  Embassy   .   .   .   .   .   *Frontispiece*

The old order in China : ox cart transport. Photograph
  by Dr. L. H. Dudley Buxton .   .   *facing page* 32

The Mongolian Steppe. Photograph by Dr. L. H.
  Dudley Buxton   164

Jacob Borodin. Photograph by Planet News Ltd.   . 214

China's Jacques Bonhomme : a typical peasant. Photograph by Dr. L. H. Dudley Buxton   .   .   . 226

Galen *alias* Blücher, Marshal of the Soviet Union and
  commander of the Soviet Far Eastern Army. Photograph by Planet News Ltd.   238

Admiral Okada, Prime Minister of Japan, 1934–6.
  Photograph by Planet News Ltd.   .   .   . 268

MAPS

Eurasia   .   .   .   .   .   *front end paper*

Pacific Ocean   .   .   .   .   *back end paper*

I

'THE FURTHER DEVELOPMENT OF THE EASTERN TRADE'

THE modern history of the Far East dates from the forcible opening of China and Japan to international trade and diplomatic intercourse in the middle decades of the nineteenth century. By the coercive intrusion of alien powers two countries, the heirs of an ancient civilization and containing within their borders a full quarter of the number of mankind, were then violently dragged from the seclusion in which they had deliberately immured themselves and driven into the bewildering arena of international affairs, the modern public world of economic interdependence and political anarchy. This opening of the gates was the beginning of a new destiny for Far Eastern lands and of a new destiny also for the Western nations by which it had been brought about; for if the former were soon involved in revolutionary changes of life and thought as a consequence of the contact with Western civilization, the latter found the Far East becoming ever more and more important in their calculations of policy, both because of the rivalry between them for power and influence in a lately opened field of commercial and financial activity and because of the new political forces set in motion within the Far East itself.

The initiative in the opening of the gates in the Far East was taken by England. It was no doubt historically inevitable that sooner or later in the nineteenth century the expansive forces of European capitalism, furnished with an ever-widening margin of superiority in armed power and with greatly improved facilities of transport, would break into the great closed market on the further side of Asia in the teeth of whatever opposition the 'native' rulers might attempt to offer. But the course of events in detail depended on when, in what circumstances, and by what nation the first serious assault was delivered. The task was not such as could be undertaken by one nation as well as another, nor could it be undertaken at all a century ago unless certain conditions had previously been fulfilled.

It was not, indeed, by any means an easy undertaking, however simple a matter it may now appear in retrospect. The problem for any European nation which might be inclined to attempt the opening of either China or Japan was that of effectively applying coercion to a large kingdom with abundant man-power and not unprovided with fire-arms at an immense distance from the homeland, and without the possibility of concentrating really large forces for a campaign. The command of the sea was assured as long as other European powers were neutral, for any European ship had been able to give the law to a junk or a prau ever since the Portuguese first penetrated into Far Eastern waters early in the sixteenth century. But naval power alone could not be expected to give a decision. The very fact that China and Japan had cut themselves off with such a degree of rigour from foreign trade made them invulnerable to the weapon of blockade, and for land operations there was no such extreme disparity between European and Asiatic forces. Finally, there was a danger that a strong initiative in the Far East by any one European state might lead to complications with other European states jealous of an advantage in which they feared they might obtain no share.

The enterprise, therefore, was too great for a small European nation, and it was not practicable for any state which did not possess suitable bases for action. Portugal, Spain, and Holland, the pioneer powers in Far Eastern trade and colonization, held bases in the East Indian islands, but all three had sunk to the level of minor powers in the European system and were primarily concerned with retaining the rights and territories they had already acquired. France after 1815 had no base for her power east of Pondicherry, and had exhausted her appetite for adventure for some time to come. Austria and Prussia were continental European powers with no Asiatic possessions; Russia possessed an empire in Asia with territory continuous from the European homeland to the shores of the Pacific, but with communications so deficient that her effective power in the Far East was very small. The U.S.A. had as yet no base near to Asia and no shipping based on Pacific coast ports before 1850; the ships from New England came to the East Indies and Canton around Cape Horn or the Cape of Good Hope. England alone between 1820 and 1840 possessed all the important qualifications for the task of gate-opening in the Far East. She had emerged from the Napoleonic wars with an undisputed naval supremacy in European waters and along the sea-way to the East, she possessed in India a base of power on a grand scale, and she had acquired in Singapore in 1819 both an advanced base suitable for the support of a 'positive' policy in the Far East and at the same time a port that was a decisive factor, by the sheer impetus of its phenomenal development as an economic centre, in the promotion of such a policy.

The British did not acquire Singapore by the purpose of the British Government of the day, but by the action of that second Clive, Sir Stamford Raffles, who refused to accept the home government's policy of withdrawal from the Malay Archipelago in favour of the Dutch. From 1794 to 1814 the domination of Holland by the French had included the Dutch among England's enemies, and in order to forestall the use of the Dutch East Indian colonies as a base for French attacks on British India, British expeditions had captured Malacca in 1795 and had occupied Java in 1811. At the Congress of Vienna in 1814, however, it was decided to make Holland, liberated from the Napoleonic empire, as strong and independent as possible in relation to France, and with this end in view England agreed to restore to her Malacca and Java. But Raffles, who had been left by Lord Minto as Lieutenant-Governor in Java, had other ideas, and so strong was his zeal for local empire-building that he even welcomed the news of Napoleon's escape from Elba. 'The wonderful and extraordinary change in the politics of Europe', he wrote at the time, 'has, with all its horrors, shed one consoling ray on this sacred Isle ; and Java may yet be permanently English.' But the Hundred Days made no difference in this respect to the arrangements which had been made at Vienna, and the Dutch were permitted to return to their former possessions, the furthest outposts of the British being now once again, as before 1795, Bengkulen on the west coast of Sumatra, and Penang on the west coast of the Malay Peninsula to the north of Malacca. In other words, the Dutch were left in control of the two vital sea passages from the Indian Ocean to the Pacific, the Sunda and Malacca Straits, and England had no station on the further side of these narrows. As a result of their better strategic position the restored Dutch were able to extend their influence over the still independent native rulers of the Archipelago to the exclusion of British trade, even though Castlereagh thought he had secured a 'direct import' for British merchants by his diplomacy.

The only way to alter this situation was to obtain a new strategic centre *inside* the Archipelago, and Raffles held the view that 'with respect to taking

possession of a vacant port, or making a treaty for
privileges with an independent chief, the prize is to
the swiftest.' Canning was opposed to any attempt
to extend British power eastward at the expense of
the Dutch, but Raffles obtained the endorsement of
Lord Hastings, the Governor-General in India, for
a scheme for 'the establishment of a station beyond
Malacca, such as may command the southern entrance of those Straits'. He founded the station in
January 1819 at Singapore at the extremity of the
Malay Peninsula on a site ceded by the Sultan of
Johore. Raffles was a Malay scholar and he was
aware from his knowledge of the history of the Archipelago that an important city had once flourished
where at the beginning of the nineteenth century
there was only a village.[1] 'But for my Malay studies,'
he writes, 'I should hardly have known that such
a place existed ; not only the European but the
Indian world was also ignorant of it.' What had
been might be again, and Raffles willed the resur-
rection of the ancient Hindu-Sumatran city with a
clear insight into its immense possibilities in the conditions of the new age, though even he could hardly
have imagined that a century after he left it—he returned to England in 1823—nearly 22 million tons
of shipping would use its harbour in a year. 'What

[1] Singapura was a colony of the Hindu kingdom of Palembang in
southern Sumatra. In the fifteenth century it was subject to Siam,
and it declined with the rise of Malacca, which was itself originally
founded by exiles from Singapura.

Malta is in the West, that may Singapore become in the East,' he wrote, and again : 'It gives us the command of China and Japan, with Siam and Cambodia, to say nothing of the islands themselves [i.e. the Malay Archipelago].'

The Dutch naturally protested at this invasion of a sphere in which they understood England to have renounced all territorial claims, and there was a chance that diplomacy in London might undo what had been done in Malaya. Even the Secret Committee of the East India Company complained that 'Sir Stamford Raffles cannot presume to suppose that he has been empowered by His Majesty's Government to make such acquisitions on behalf of the Crown'. But a friend in London assured Raffles that a powerful clique was working for ' the further development of the Eastern trade', and it was soon apparent that Singapore, if not Java, was to be 'permanently English'. The port was a success from the beginning and its prosperity grew by leaps and bounds. An ardent free-trade enthusiast, Raffles had declared Singapore 'a free port and the trade thereof open to ships and vessels of every nation, free of duty, equally and alike to all'. In 1824 the port was used by 35,000 tonnage of shipping, in 1835 by 200,000. So commerce grew and increased its appetite with what it fed on, until the accumulated force of economic development was sufficient to give a new directive to political power and to burst open the gates of foreigner-excluding China.

The acquisition of Singapore is historically most important as the decisive move in the advance of the European maritime powers towards the central region of the Far East, but it has to be remembered that the primary intention of the enterprise was to break the Dutch commercial monopoly in the Malay archipelago. The decision of this ancient quarrel is also important for more recent history because the settlement of colonial claims that was then made has ever since provided (subject to a few unimportant modifications) a stable and undisputed element in the Far Eastern situation. The Anglo-Dutch agreement of 1824 meant at once a solution of old problems in this part of the world and an emergence of new ones with a different geographical focus. For over three centuries from the Portuguese capture of Malacca in 1511 the traffic of the East Indian islands had been the main objective and bone of contention for the European maritime powers in the seas beyond the Indian Ocean. These islands were nearer than China and Japan on the sea-way round Asia, their numerous petty native sovereignties offered easier opportunities for intrigue and coercion than the bigger and more strongly organized kingdoms to the north, and above all they contained the principal or only area of production of some of the most valuable spices on the list of European demand. The spice trade, by its exceptional development in an age of scanty capital and small turnover and by the limitation of the source of supply to a remote region, lent itself to monopoly, and became a factor in general history to an extent that is hard to imagine in our time. It was above all to break the Egyptian-Venetian middleman monopoly of the spice trade that the Portuguese made their way round Africa into the Indian Ocean. It was to break the subsequent Portuguese monopoly that the Dutch (who had been distributors for the Portuguese until Lisbon was closed against them in 1594) sailed to the sources of supply; and it was the raising of the price of pepper against London by the Dutch that led to the incorporation of the English East India Company in 1600. Of the various spices in demand pepper and ginger could be obtained from India and Ceylon, but cloves and nutmegs came almost entirely from the Moluccas, and it was thither that a Portuguese squadron was dispatched immediately after Albuquerque's capture of Malacca in 1511. With the arrival of the Dutch and English in the Indies a three-cornered struggle for supremacy began, and in the course of the seventeenth century resulted in the defeat of Portugal in both Indian and Indonesian waters, with the victory of England in the former and of Holland in the latter. The English, after their expulsion from Bantam in 1682, concentrated their energies in India and until 1795 had no foothold in the Archipelago except Bengkulen. Then in the age of the French Revolutionary wars the English went east to destroy the empire of a Holland which had become the vassal of France. The settle-

ment of 1814 restored this empire to the Dutch, but
it failed to reverse entirely the decision of events,
for there was no longer a sufficient basis of strength
for the Dutch position. In the seventeenth century
the Dutch had expelled their rivals by sheer force ;
in 1814 they were given back their lost Far Eastern
colonies only as an act of policy on the part of
stronger powers who were seeking counter-weights to
a beaten but still formidable France. Their tenure
was thus by favour, and they were presuming on the
forbearance of the British Government when they attempted to pursue a monopolist policy in areas where
trading privileges had been conceded to British merchants by native rulers. Raffles called this bluff by
his expedition through the Straits of Malacca. The
real weakness of the Dutch was exposed in their
failure to use force against the intruders ; 'I no
more trouble my head about the Dutch', wrote
Raffles soon after his successful *coup*.

By the Anglo-Dutch agreement of 1824 Dutch
Malacca was exchanged for British Bengkulen, the
Dutch renounced all claims to supremacy in the
Malay Peninsula, and the English made a corresponding renunciation for Sumatra (except Achin in the
extreme north, which remained under British protection until 1872). A considerable trade was meanwhile developing between Singapore and the northern
coast of Borneo which was more accessible from
Malaya than from the centres of Dutch power in
Java and Celebes, and a belt of British-protected

territory, comprising British North Borneo, Brunei and Sarawak, was gradually formed, the boundary between British and Dutch Borneo being at last fixed by a treaty in 1891. Elsewhere in the islands the Dutch were left with a free hand, and in the end they established their territorial sovereignty over the whole of Indonesia west of New Guinea and south of the Philippines, with the exception of the British sphere in northern Borneo and the eastern half of the island of Timor, which was retained by Portugal as a memorial of her former empire. To-day the Dutch hold in the East Indies a colonial domain with more than sixty times the area and seven and a quarter times the population of the home country—a not unsatisfactory result of three centuries of imperialist competition for a power which has long been of minor rank in European affairs.

It was not, however, the Malay Archipelago that was to be the subject of the Far Eastern Question in the middle and later decades of the nineteenth century. The treaty of 1824 yielded a permanent settlement of outstanding issues between England and Holland, but it did not inaugurate an age of peace and tranquillity in the Far East; only, the scene of conflict was now removed northward from the Equator up the Pacific coast of the mainland of Asia. In 1840, twenty-one years after the acquisition of Singapore, England was at war with China.

II

THE OPENING OF THE GATES

THE situation with regard to China from the point of view of European merchants remained in the early nineteenth century essentially what it had been in 1627, when the Presidency of Batavia declared in a memorandum to the Directors of the East India Company: 'Concerning the Trade of China, three things are especially made known unto the World. The One is, the abundant trade it affordeth. The Second is, that they admit no Stranger into their country. The Third is, that Trade is as Life unto the Vulgar, which in remote parts they will seek and accommodate, with Hazard of all they have.' The picture thus drawn continued to represent China as it appeared to foreigners during the next two centuries—a country of immense commercial possibilities with a population anxious to trade with foreigners but prevented from so doing by the monstrous perversity of its rulers. The Imperial Court, indeed, permitted a foreign trade to grow up, but it was confined by law after 1757 to a single port (Canton) and subject to so many irksome restrictions and regulations that it became almost as great a source of grievances as complete seclusion would have been.

From the Chinese point of view none of the foreigners' grievances could have any validity, because the premise of Chinese thinking with regard to foreign relations was a political ideal totally different from that of the Europeans. The Chinese had no conception of a world of equal sovereign states maintaining permanent diplomatic relations with one another or of international trade as a natural and normal part of economic life implying a system of rights and duties everywhere valid. Ideally China was the legitimate world-state, coextensive with true civilization and economically self-contained. If foreigners were allowed to trade in Chinese ports it was a revocable privilege imposing no obligations of any kind on China. China did not seek foreign trade, and did not invite foreign traders to come to her shores. If they came, they must be prepared to submit to whatever treatment was meted out to them, and if they did not like it, they could go. The Chinese Government always maintained that the country had no need of external commerce and could easily dispense with it if it became a source of trouble. As the Emperor Ch'ien Lung declared in his 'mandate' to King George III of England delivered to Lord Macartney's embassy in 1793, 'The Celestial Empire possesses all things in prolific abundance and lacks no product within its borders. There is therefore no need to import the manufactures of outside barbarians in exchange for our own products.'

This attitude of indifference to foreign trade was indeed a reflection of the fact that in the eighteenth century there was hardly any market for European goods in China. In 1702 the supercargoes of a ship visiting Canton had to report: 'Our Europe goods in no demand, particularly Cloth and Perpetuanoes; of which remained in Town, unsold, all that were brought this three Years past.' As the European demand for tea (of which China was then the only source) rapidly grew during the eighteenth century, while there was little increase in the Chinese demand for European goods, the China trade became more and more unbalanced, and the English East India Company had constantly to choose between making large purchases of silver and selling English manufactured goods at a loss. Searching for a commodity which could be sold at a profit in China, the Company discovered the merits of opium, of which it held a monopoly in Bengal. This was a solution of the economic problem, but it raised fresh difficulties between the traders and the Chinese authorities, for the importation of the drug was prohibited by a series of Imperial edicts, and the trade could, therefore, only be carried on by smuggling with the collusion of corrupt local officials. The attempt made by Lin Tse-hsü in 1839 to enforce the prohibition law by the confiscation of stocks of opium, valued at over £1,250,000, from British merchants at Canton provided the occasion for the outbreak of the First Anglo-Chinese War.

The dispute about opium, however, merely brought to a head a conflict with regard to the general conditions of trade which had been developing for many years. It was indeed only a matter of time before the radical divergence of policies must lead to a clash in which force would be employed. Early in the eighteenth century the English traders had already the will, if not the power, to use it, and in 1721 in protest against the arrest of some sailors in Canton the supercargoes of the *Cadogan* warned the Hoppo [1] that 'as His Majesty the King of England has several Men of War about Madras and other places in the East Indies, we cannot answer what may be the consequences of such a procedure as the denying us that justice which we demand'. This was really an idle threat in 1721, but such language had a reality of power behind it a century later, and the traders were conscious of the ultimate strength of their position. In the words of Sir Ernest Satow,[2] 'the Englishmen who went to Canton from India belonged to a race that had just emerged triumphantly from a great war in Europe; and they were accustomed to domineer over Asiatics'.

The conditions of the China trade were certainly such as to inflict the maximum of humiliation, inconvenience, and hazard on those Europeans who took part in it. The foreign traders were confined to a plot of ground of a few acres at Canton; they were not allowed to visit any other port or to travel or reside in the interior or even to enter the city of Canton itself. They could deal only with a licensed

---

[1] 'Hoppo' was the English rendering of a Cantonese abbreviation of the title *Yüeh hai kuan pu*—Superintendent of Yüeh Sea Customs.

[2] Chap. XXVIII, p. 803, of *The Cambridge Modern History*, vol. xi.

guild of Chinese merchants, and they could hold communication with the Chinese officials only through the medium of this guild. There was no fixed tariff, but the trade was subject to various charges the amount of which was essentially a matter of bargaining. Foreigners were subject to Chinese law, the principles and administration of which were often contrary to their ideas of justice, and as they had no diplomatic or consular representation, there was no way in which their grievances could be officially discussed and remedied.[1]

The situation grew worse with the abolition by England of the East India Company's monopoly of the China trade in 1834. Hitherto the Company as a unit had dealt with the Chinese merchant guild, but now with a number of competing firms and no monopolist organization to accept responsibility for the English community it became necessary to have someone at Canton to perform the functions of a consul. For this purpose Lord Napier was sent out with the title of Superintendent of Trade. He failed, however, to obtain any recognition of his official status from the Chinese authorities, and the Viceroy finally ordered him to leave Canton, declaring that 'the petty affairs of commerce are to be settled by

[1] Two embassies had been sent from England to Peking with the object of securing greater facilities for trade and, if possible, establishing permanent diplomatic relations—one under Lord Macartney in 1792 and another under Lord Amherst in 1816. Neither of them met with any success, though Macartney was received in audience by the Emperor Ch'ien Lung.

the merchants themselves; officials have nothing to hear on the subject'. As the expulsion order was accompanied by a threat to stop the trade altogether, Napier withdrew to Macao, where he died in the same year (1834). Before his death he recommended to London the dispatch of an expedition to China and the seizure of the island of Hong Kong, but no action was taken by the British Government until 1838, when, Palmerston being Foreign Secretary, a naval squadron was sent to Chinese waters. Hostilities broke out during the following year after Lin's confiscation of the opium stocks at Canton.

Two years of desultory warfare, in which the Chinese everywhere suffered defeat, led to the signing of the Treaty of Nanking in 1842. By the terms of this treaty Hong Kong was ceded to the victors, four more ports in addition to Canton—namely, Amoy, Foochow, Ningpo, and Shanghai, were opened to foreign trade and residence, the monopoly of the Chinese 'hong' merchants was abolished, consuls were to be appointed in the five ports with the right to deal directly with the provincial authorities, and merchandise was to be subject to no charges over and above a 'fair and regular' tariff, which was fixed at 5 per cent. *ad valorem*. A supplementary agreement in 1843 added two provisions which have been of the greatest importance in subsequent history—most-favoured-nation treatment and extraterritorial jurisdiction of consuls.

The British had announced when they went to

war with China that whatever new commercial advantages they might obtain thereby would be open to all other nations. After the Treaty of Nanking, therefore, other states soon approached China with a view to concluding similar treaties, and fearing that rival Powers which had not made war on China would take the opportunity to gain by intrigue privileges which had not been accorded to victorious might, the British insisted on a guarantee that they would also obtain any advantage or right granted to any other nation in China. After 1843 a most-favoured-nation clause was inserted in most of the treaties made by foreign Powers with China; the original intention was to ensure that the Chinese market should be open to all on equal terms, but its effect was to establish a common front of the foreign Powers in making demands on China, since whatever was granted to one became available to all, no matter what had been the circumstances or conditions of the first grant.

The extraterritorial jurisdiction of consuls was introduced to meet the grievances of the traders who had been subject to Chinese law. The system was not at first regarded as a serious restriction of China's sovereignty, as the Consuls accepted responsibility for the behaviour of their nationals, who were confined to the five 'treaty ports', and by the withdrawal of foreigners from the jurisdiction of Chinese courts a major source of friction with the Chinese authorities seemed to have been eliminated. But with the later multiplication of treaty ports and the concession to foreigners of the right to travel in the interior, many abuses crept in, and the Chinese state was gravely embarrassed by the presence within its borders of large numbers of aliens over whom it had no control, but whose lives and property it was strictly bound to protect.

A development, not necessarily involved in the grant of extraterritorial rights to foreigners, but arising out of it, was the growth of autonomous foreign 'settlements', some of which became virtually city-states within, but not of, the Chinese empire. The foreign 'settlements' were a natural result of the conditions prevailing in China. By the Treaty of Nanking and treaties subsequently concluded with Powers other than England, foreigners had the right to reside in the 'treaty ports'. But the Chinese officials, to whom their presence was an abomination, sought to keep them as far as possible apart from the mass of the population and guard the Chinese heritage from their contaminating influence. The foreigners for their part were not anxious to live scattered about within the crowded walled cities, where the 'medieval' ways of living were distasteful to them and they would have, whatever might be their treaty rights, no security against popular manifestations of hostility. It was in the interest of both parties, therefore, to arrange for leases of suburban land on which the foreigners could erect houses for themselves and live under the jurisdiction of their

consuls and the protection of their own police. But
these settlements, originally intended as residential
quarters, became in some cases economic centres
superseding the old Chinese cities to which they were
attached. The business facilities they provided and
their immunity from the exactions of Chinese officialdom and from looting in time of civil disturbance
attracted Chinese merchants and bankers, and they
grew into distinct urban units with continuing foreign
administration but large majorities of Chinese inhabitants. The most striking example of the evolution of the extraterritorial settlement town was at
Shanghai, which had been a comparatively small
place as long as China's foreign trade was confined to
Canton, but rapidly rose to the position of the chief
port of the empire after foreign shipping was allowed
direct access to the Yangtse delta. The great increase of traffic centred, not on the old Chinese city,
but on the waterfront of the foreign settlements
lower down the Whangpoo river. The British and
American holdings were united and thrown open to
all comers, forming the present International Settlement ; only the French retained a distinct settlement
of their own. There was an enormous influx of
Chinese into the two settlements, the population within their boundaries at the present day being about
1,300,000 Chinese to less than 50,000 foreigners. As a
result of this historical development, Shanghai with
a total population of three and a half millions, making
it the fifth largest city of the world, is divided into

three separate administrative areas—the International Settlement, the French Concession, and Chinese Greater Shanghai. The first two of these are still under foreign rule, control in municipal affairs being retained by an electorate of foreign ratepayers, though a limited representation has been conceded to Chinese residents since 1926. The situation which now exists is something which could not have been conceived by the first British Consul, Captain Balfour, who in 1843 fixed the limits of what was to be the British Settlement in the mud flats in the angle between the Whangpoo and Soochow Creek.

The treaty limitation of the tariff was also a provision of the new system destined to create trouble in the future. It deprived China of tariff autonomy at a time when the new conditions and problems confronting the state required an increase of revenue for the central government and Customs duties were the most obvious source for the relief of the treasury. Further, it operated in favour of the foreign trader as opposed to the Chinese, for treaty rates were extended to coastwise and inland traffic, and foreigners thus had a guaranteed immunity from those exactions of local officials to which their Chinese competitors remained liable.

The financial needs of the central government reconciled it to the existence of the treaty ports, and induced it not only to open new ports to trade on demand but even to open some on its own initiative. There were still three claims of foreigners, however,

E

which the Court of Peking would not yield except to
force: one was the right to travel freely in the interior
of China, the second was the right to have diplomatic
representatives stationed in Peking on terms of
equality with the Chinese sovereign, and the third
was the right of missionaries to propagate Christianity with a legal guarantee of toleration for their
converts.

Surrender on these three points was exacted from
China by the war of 1856–60. The war began with
a dispute over the extent of extraterritorial jurisdiction. The British attacked Canton when the Viceroy
declined to make an apology for the boarding of a
vessel flying the British flag by Chinese police in
search of alleged pirates. The British were joined
in war against China by France, the Anglo-French
combination established in the Crimean war being
thus transferred to the Far East. France acted
avowedly as protector of Catholic missions, a rôle
undertaken by the French Second Empire as part
of Napoleon III's endeavour to win the support of
the Catholic Church. The pretext for the campaign
against China was the execution of the French missionary Chapdelaine in Kwangsi.[1] The French also

---

[1] Before the signing of the Tientsin Treaty of 1858 missionaries had
no legal right to travel outside the five Treaty Ports. Chinese officials
could arrest any foreigners found outside these cities and return them
to their consuls, but the missionaries came out of the Treaty Ports
again as fast as they were sent back, and the officials could not im-
prison or kill them as they were protected by extraterritorial jurisdiction. Kwangsi was at this time ravaged by the Christian T'ai P'ing

invaded Annam in 1858 in co-operation with a Spanish expedition from the Philippines to procure toleration for Catholicism in that country, and by annexing part of it laid the foundations for a colonial empire destined to swallow it completely.

After a series of naval and military operations, the climax of which was a march to Peking, the allies obtained from China satisfaction for all their demands plus a considerable indemnity. To enable China to pay the indemnity, and to save the central government from bankruptcy (the T'ai P'ing rebellion having cut off a great part of its revenue while the war was in progress) without increasing the tariff, the Maritime Customs were placed by treaty under the control of a Foreign Inspectorate, thus extending to all ports as a permanent institution a system adopted as a temporary expedient at Shanghai in 1854.

China's seclusion was a thing of the past after 1860. The opening of the gates had been accomplished by two wars, in the first of which England alone, and in the second England and France together, applied coercion to China. Meanwhile the Americans had forced the opening of Japan by a naval demonstration, but without actual fighting. The geographical position of Japan determined the relative pressure of the Western Powers upon her. Japan was more remote than China as approached

rebels, and the provincial authorities suspected all Christian propagandists of sedition.

from the Indian Ocean, but nearer to America across the Pacific. For three decades before 1850 the Americans had had an important whaling industry in the northern Pacific, and had made several unsuccessful attempts to obtain facilities for the whalers in Japan. When the development of direct shipping between San Francisco and Shanghai put Japan in the path of an important trade route, the need for a port of call in Japan was still more strongly felt, and this special incentive was added to the general desire of the maritime Powers to break down all barriers to trade. Japan had adopted seclusionism in an extreme form, for not only was trade confined to a single port (Nagasaki), but it was restricted to two nations, the Chinese and the Dutch. It was obvious, however, that after China had failed to maintain the seclusion policy, Japan with her much greater vulnerability to naval aggression could not hope to hold out for long. The Dutch themselves, aware that they had not the power to hold their monopoly —which was in any case of small value in consequence of the conditions imposed on the trade at Nagasaki—urged the Japanese Government to open the country. A letter transmitted from the Colonial Minister of the Netherlands in 1844 pointed out by way of warning that 'to reject intercourse necessarily creates enemies' and that China, having tried to pursue such a policy, had just been decisively defeated in war by England. The rulers of Japan were not persuaded by the general arguments in favour of renouncing the seclusion policy, but they were impressed by the effectiveness of Western military power as revealed in the war of 1839–42, and it was probably this example more than anything else which deterred them from any attempt at resistance when Commodore Perry arrived in Uraga Bay in 1853 with a squadron of four warships, including a steam frigate, and pressed for a 'treaty of amity and commerce'. To gain time and to distribute responsibility for the capitulation, the government of the Shogunate at Yedo, which had long been *de facto* the supreme authority in Japan, though nominally holding power only by delegation from the Emperor in Kyoto, pleaded to Perry that it must consult the Emperor and the feudal lords before taking a decision of such importance. Perry then sailed away, saying he would return in the following year. When he reappeared, the number of his ships had been raised from four to seven, and it was later increased to nine. With this imposing demonstration of force he obtained the opening of two ports to American shipping and trade and the right to representation by a consul. A few months later Admiral Sir James Stirling with four warships sailed to Nagasaki and secured a similar treaty for England.

In 1858, when China was again defeated in war by Western military art, powerful English and French forces were gathered in the Far East, ready to impose terms not only on China but also on Japan. This situation led the *Shogun*'s government to conclude a series of treaties greatly extending the breach in the old seclusion policy, so that once again the spectacle of China's disaster caused Japan to yield without actual war. Hostilities did occur, however, during the next few years, though they involved only individual magnates of the Japanese feudal system and not the central government. A British squadron bombarded Kagoshima, the capital of the Satsuma fief, in 1863, in order to obtain satisfaction for the killing of an Englishman by Satsuma soldiers. In the following year a joint expedition of British, French, Dutch, and American warships attacked Shimonoseki in order to open the Straits, which had been closed by the lord of Choshu in response to orders from the Imperial Court for the 'expulsion of the barbarians' from Japan. As these orders had come from Kyoto, and as the Emperor had never ratified the treaties with foreign Powers which the Shogun had concluded, the squadrons of the four nations sailed to Osaka Bay in the summer of 1865 and demanded the Imperial ratification, which was then given. This was the last occasion on which the Western Powers had to threaten violence in order to overcome the resistance of anti-foreign seclusionism in Japan. Henceforth Japan was to follow the path of voluntary self-modernization, simultaneously satisfying the Western Powers by the development of commercial facilities and laying the foundations for her own emergence as a formidable modern state.

III

THE WESTERNIZERS

IN the period between 1839 and 1865 we find China and Japan reacting similarly to the pressure put upon them by the trade-seeking Western Powers. Both countries are opened by *force majeure* to international commercial and diplomatic intercourse; in both the ruling classes are imbued with a fanatical conservatism and intense anti-foreign feeling; in both there is the will to resist and to 'expel the barbarians' without the means to put the will into effect, so that the appeal to arms only brings defeat and additional exactions. In the period of the opening of the gates China and Japan are confronted with the same situation and react to it, broadly speaking, in the same way. But after 1865 there is a steadily increasing divergence. Japan passes under the control of a group of statesmen who strive with impatient energy to re-form the institutions of their country in imitation of the West, while the Court and bureaucracy of China cling to the lost cause which they are neither willing to renounce nor able to defend. From this divergence of policies springs the Far Eastern Question as it has existed since 1894, the problem created by the continuing 'backwardness' and weakness of China.

The explanation of the striking contrast between China and Japan in the last thirty years of the nineteenth century is to be sought in the different social and political institutions existing in the two countries before the violent invasion of the Western Powers. Briefly, it may be said, in the first place, that the social ascendancy of a military caste in Japan was a factor in favour of change, because the argument of military defeat was for its members convincing as a refutation of conservatism, whereas it was not convincing for the class of 'scholars' supreme in Chinese society; and secondly, that the remarkable dual system of government in Japan was conducive to an alliance between the legitimate monarchy and revolutionary forces to the great advantage of both, whereas in China the Court was inseparably bound up with reactionary vested interests.

The ruling class in China was defined, not by nobility of birth or by property, but by a special type of education and cultural attainment. In early times the structure of Chinese society had been rigidly aristocratic, but the centralizing monarchy had striven to create a bureaucratic administration superior to provincial and clan loyalties, and for this purpose had gradually evolved the system of recruiting the civil service by means of public competitive examinations in classical learning, open to anyone who could obtain an education. The effect of this was to break down hereditary divisions of status and to confer the highest social prestige on the class of scholars from whose ranks the governing officials were drawn.

Politically, the common culture imposed on aspirants to office all over the country by the examination system, combined with the rule that officials did not serve in the provinces in which they were born, produced a degree of national unity and coherence of 'public opinion' very remarkable for a country of vast area, poor communications, and localized patriarchal family life.

The class of scholars was in effect a clergy, and its religion was identical with the original cultural tradition of China, scholastically elaborated and given a rigid doctrinal form. This religion is known to foreigners as Confucianism, but was in China more commonly known simply as the *Ju chiao* or 'scholars' teaching', the terms 'scholar' and 'Confucian' having become synonymous.[1] The civil service examinations required the study of certain classical texts, proficiency in essay-writing according to approved literary models, and acceptance of the orthodox interpretation of Confucian philosophy as determined by the 'schoolmen' of the Sung dynasty. The system was an imposing and effective cultural-political creation, but it was fatal to independence of thought, and it is worthy of note that the finest literary and artistic achievements of the Chinese genius belong to periods before the institution assumed its final,

[1] This is as if Christianity had been called in Europe the 'clergy's teaching'. There is an analogy in so far as English usage normally assumes that 'the churches' and 'the clergy' mean Christian churches and clergy, though the terms are sometimes used for the organizations and professional ministers of non-Christian religions.

F

stereotyped form. By the nineteenth century it had produced an extreme narrowness and conservatism of outlook in the governing bureaucracy. As C. P. Fitzgerald remarks : [1]

'Trained in a classical tradition which excluded all consideration of non-Confucian philosophy, and chosen by a highly competitive examination based upon the most conventional interpretation of that philosophy, the type of mind that entered the civil service was a mind closed to all idea of progress, almost incapable of grasping the possibility, still less the need, for change. The men who rebelled against this training or found this tradition unsatisfying, did not succeed in these specialised examinations, or if they occasionally passed into the civil service, they found the atmosphere so uncongenial that they either resigned, or were relegated to unimportant posts where they exercised no influence. The system was self-perpetuating, seemingly immutable.'

With such a training and outlook the scholar-officials or 'mandarins' [2] of China were men who regarded themselves as concerned primarily with maintaining intact a certain religious and cultural tradition and only secondarily with secular administration. This meant that they regarded defeat in war, and even foreign conquest, as less of a disaster than the introduction of new or alien customs and ideas into the body cultural of China. For them it

---

[1] *China: a Short Cultural History* (Cresset Historical Series), p. 543.
[2] From the Portuguese *mandar*, a term applied by the foreign merchants to all Chinese officials entitled to wear buttons denoting degrees of rank on their hats.

would be the greatest treason to allow innovations destructive of Confucian doctrine and practice merely in order to increase the military strength of the state or the economic prosperity of the people. It is of course easy to exaggerate the indifference to military affairs characteristic of the scholar class. Under the native Chinese dynasties, such as the T'ang, Sung, and Ming, great attention had been given to military problems, and the early Ming Emperors in particular had been great fighters and conquerors. But in the seventeenth century the Manchus, a barbarous, semi-nomadic people from what is now Kirin province, had succeeded in conquering China by intervening in a civil war after the overthrow by rebellion of the Ming dynasty. The Manchus, maintained in garrisons drawing tribute from China, were until the end of the eighteenth century the effective standing army of the Manchu-Chinese empire thus formed. The civil administration, on the other hand, continued to be dominated by Chinese, selected as under the Ming by the examination system, and the Manchu princes and courtiers 'became more Chinese than the Chinese themselves'. The effect of the Manchu ascendancy was not only to make the Chinese scholar class more essentially civilian and unmilitary than it had formerly been, but also to nourish the idea that the one thing needful was the preservation of Confucian orthodoxy and that all else was of lesser consequence.

When, therefore, the European intruders demonstrated the superiority of their military art in the war of 1839–42 and compelled the opening of new ports to trade, it was not at all obvious to the Chinese official mind that the time-honoured institutions of the Middle Kingdom must be transformed and adapted to the task of coping with the new swarm of seafaring barbarians who had replaced the earlier Malay and Japanese corsairs as the nuisance of the south coast. It was agreed that measures must be taken to repel the barbarians, but military efficiency was not to be gained at the cost of adulterating the pure word of Confucian learning with Western science or changing the habits of the people by a wholesale introduction of Western forms of economic and political organization.

The prevailing attitude of mind among the scholar-officials is clearly shown in the controversy that went on about maritime defence during and just after the Opium War. The Emperor Tao Kuang was extremely annoyed at the successive defeats of his forces by the English, and he issued a number of edicts which show a will to accept innovations. In a decree of July 1842 he declared:

'In my opinion, what the rebellious barbarians rely on is the fact that Chinese war junks are incapable of going out to sea to fight them; therefore they do what they please without any fear. If Fukien, Chekiang and Kwangtung each can build large-sized warships with many more guns on board, they will be able to fight the rebellious barbarians on the sea.'

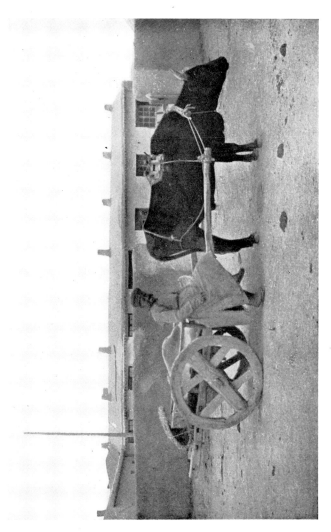

THE OLD ORDER IN CHINA: OX CART TRANSPORT

Another Imperial edict, issued soon after the conclusion of the Nanking Treaty, ordered a reorganization of coastal defence and declared: 'The size,
structure and equipment of warships . . . must not
be confined to the old methods and conventional
practice.' The Governor of Chekiang, however, re-
ported against the building of ships of foreign design
which had already been begun at Canton. 'China',
he wrote, 'has very little strong timber and no ship-
wrights of suitable skill. If we hastily imitate foreign
ships they cannot be as strong, and if we could build
them equally strong, they would be no good because
nobody knows how to use them.' Arguments of this
type carried the day, and the schemes for improving
the navy were abandoned, so that China was no
more prepared for effective resistance in the war of
1856 than she had been in 1839. The stumbling-
block was the question of technical training, which
could only be obtained from foreigners, and which
would be a channel for letting into China all kinds
of foreign fashions and ideas.

The antagonism of the Confucian *literati* to strange
customs and heterodox thinking was greatly aggravated by the propaganda of Christian missions.
There would have been objection enough to the
influence of alien ideas even if the foreign penetration into China had been of a purely secular kind,
but the opposition was inevitably far more uncompromising and fanatical when the Western nations
and their civilization were associated with the zealous

propagation of an alien religion. Confucianism was up to a point a tolerant faith. It gave scope in China for popular cults, Taoist or Buddhist, which it regarded as harmless and which were often blended with it in the religious belief and practice of individuals. But it persecuted religions which were regarded as subversive and incompatible with its ideology. Certain Buddhist sects came under the ban and so also did Islam and Christianity. Events after the middle of the nineteenth century appeared to give confirmation to the worst fears and suspicions of the Confucians with regard to Christianity. In the first place, it became identified with violent revolution; the great T'ai P'ing insurrection, which involved China in a devastating thirteen-year civil war, was emphatically a Christian movement. It rallied to itself diverse forces of social discontent and the strong anti-Manchu sentiment of the southern provinces, but the inspiration of its leaders was a peculiar form of Christianity founded on the teachings of the Protestant missionaries. The leader of the revolt, Hung Hsiu-ch'üan, proclaimed himself at once a divinely inspired prophet, the 'Younger Brother of Jesus', and the founder of a new dynasty of temporal monarchs. The T'ai P'ings were violently intolerant; they persecuted Buddhists, Taoists, and sometimes even Roman Catholics as idolaters, and claimed to have superseded the Confucian classics by their new revelation.

Fitzgerald rightly points out that 'in European

histories of China the political character of the T'ai
P'ing rebellion is emphasized, and the religious side
is either misrepresented or derided. Yet to the T'ai
P'ing leaders themselves it was their faith which
mattered even more than victory over the Manchus.
Had they abandoned their religious convictions and
directed their efforts to raising a national revolt their
success would have been assured.' The civil war
had indeed the character of a war of religion, and it
is not surprising that the result of this episode was
to intensify the hostility of the Confucians towards
the Western world and all its works. The foreign
missionaries (though not all of them) might disown
the persecuting zeal of the T'ai P'ings and denounce
their strange theology, and the movement was
actually suppressed with the aid of the Christian
Powers themselves (from motives of political calculation), but the fact remained that the movement
arose as a result of missionary propaganda and provided a foretaste of what was to be expected from
an extension of that influence.

With the memory of the T'ai P'ing rebellion fresh
in their minds, the Confucian scholar-officials found
themselves in the sixties rendered impotent by
treaties imposed on China to check the systematic
propagation of what they regarded as a pernicious
doctrine. The treaties of 1858 and 1860, extorted
from China by war, not only gave the Christian missionaries the legal right to preach their religion
throughout the length and breadth of the land with

the extraterritorial immunity belonging to all foreigners, but also placed their converts under the protection of foreign Powers, by giving them a treaty guarantee against persecution, official or unofficial. This protectorate of converts 'tended to remove Chinese Christians from the jurisdiction of their government and to make of Christian communities *imperia in imperio*, widely scattered enclaves under the defence of aliens'. [1] Disputes and conflicts arising out of the toleration clauses of the treaties, with frequent anti-Christian rioting and bloodshed, went on throughout the last four decades of the nineteenth century, and kept the Confucians in a mood of die-hard opposition to every manifestation of Western cultural influence.

In Japan a very different development was meanwhile taking place, and its origin can be traced to the significant difference of social structure which has already been indicated. In Japan, as in China, the officially approved 'learning' in the early nineteenth century was Confucian, but the competitive examination system had never been established there, and social supremacy belonged, not to the scholar as such, but to the military noble. The upper social class in Japan was divided into three grades: first, the *kuge* or Court nobles, an exclusive circle of about one hundred and fifty families claiming descent from collateral branches of the Imperial dynasty; second, the *daimyo* or feudal lords, number-

[1] K. S. Latourette, *A History of Christian Missions in China*, p. 279.

ing more than two hundred and fifty families, with whom may be reckoned the more numerous minor gentry called *hatamoto*; third, the *samurai* or hereditary retainers of the feudal lords, supported by the latter from the revenues of their fiefs. The *samurai* were a numerous class and were divided into groups corresponding to the fiefs they inhabited and the lords to whom they owed allegiance. These groups are conventionally termed 'clans' in English usage relating to Japan. The *daimyo* and the *samurai* together formed the *buke* or military caste, originally differentiated as such at a time when the *kuge* were the governing aristocracy, confining themselves to the offices of the civil administration and leaving military service to the lesser nobility. As a result of centuries of social evolution the *kuge* had been reduced to penury and only survived as a class because of the prestige of the Imperial dynasty, while virtually all the land in the country had passed into the hands of the *daimyo* aristocracy and was held by military tenure.

The *kuge*, confined to Kyoto and excluded from offices other than those of the secluded Imperial Court, had little influence in spite of their exalted rank. The *daimyo*, who were nominally rulers of their fiefs, and a group of whom filled the higher offices of the central government, had mostly become *fainéants* during the long period of peace and security since 1615. The administration of the country, both central and local, was actually in the hands of the *samurai,* who formed the real governing class. There was, however, a sharp divergence of interest between the section of this class belonging to clans in direct vassalage to the house of Tokugawa, which held the Shogunate, the *de facto* national monarchy, and that belonging to the so-called *tozama* or 'outside' clans. The former group staffed the bureaucracy of the Shogunate, which, although it had little control over the domestic affairs of the fiefs, had the direct administration of the five 'Imperial cities'—Kyoto, Yedo, Osaka, Sakai, and Nagasaki—and thus provided very lucrative appointments. The 'outside' clans of *samurai* were, as a result of this system of privilege, led by men who had had considerable political experience in semi-sovereign government, but were bitterly dissatisfied with the existing political order and anxious for an opportunity to subvert it. The curious, centrally controlled feudalism of the Tokugawa system was in fact only kept going by the method of hostage-taking devised to subdue the *daimyo* after the civil war in which the Tokugawa faction triumphed over their opponents. All the feudal lords had to keep their families in Yedo, the centre of the Tokugawa power, and to reside there themselves for a part of each year. By such a measure the Tokugawa Shoguns repressed feudal anarchy for two and a half centuries without either producing a centralized state or conciliating the 'outside' clans. This fact is highly significant for an understanding of modern Japan.

The social system above described was far less resistant to 'westernizing' reforms than the Chinese. The Japanese upper class, defined by birth, was indeed much narrower in its social basis than the Chinese scholar class which was continually recruited from the mass of the people. It would have offered a strong resistance to any attempt to make a revolution from below, to transfer power to the despised *heimin* or commoners, the 'Third Estate' of Japanese feudalism, including peasants, artisans, and merchants. But no such social revolution was involved in reforms designed to turn Japan into a centralized national state, and the hereditary definitions of Japanese society were in effect an aid to the reformers. The status of a Japanese noble, being derived from family descent, was not necessarily impaired by the adoption of Western habits and ideas (the examples of England and Germany being evidence that these could coexist with a very large element of aristocratic privilege, formal or informal), whereas the status of the Chinese mandarin was wholly bound up with that Confucian learning to which his class owed its *raison d'être*.

The Confucian scholar, moreover, denied the whole past of China if he discarded the pattern of the civilization which embodied the history of his race from earliest recorded times. The Japanese reformer felt no such sense of cultural treason. In borrowing from the West Japan did no more than she had previously done in borrowing from China; China, on the other hand, had no precedent for such borrowing—for the reception of Buddhism in China had not affected the supremacy of the older Confucian tradition. China regarded herself as the original source of all wisdom. In Japanese culture there was nothing purely original and native to the country (not taking into account the original variations which have been made by the Japanese on Chinese themes) except the old national religious cult known as Shinto and the prehistorically founded Imperial dynasty which was glorified by its mythology. This pre-Chinese, exclusively Japanese, element had been so far submerged in the course of centuries by Chinese modes and fashions that in the nineteenth century it had become a factor subversive of the *status quo* and was ready for combination with the new Westernism in a common cause of national independence and Imperial restoration.

The established civilization of Japan was thus relatively pervious to Western influences since it was neither bound up with the very definition of the socially dominant class, nor was it in the main indigenous. But the strongest positive factor in converting the *samurai* to an admiration and envy of things Western—a factor inoperative in China—was the reaction of an intense martial pride to the defeats inflicted by the superior armaments of Western nations. The Chinese bureaucrat was not unduly perturbed by the British victories in the Opium War. China had been many times invaded, and twice completely conquered, by nomads from the north, and the power of British warships and cannon was no more a proof of civilization than the prowess of Mongol or Manchu cavalry. The ravages of barbarians were of minor importance as long as a proper reverence for ancient tradition was maintained in the Middle Kingdom. But Japan had never in historic times been successfully invaded by an alien enemy, and the country's helplessness in the face of the fort-blasting gunfire of the 'black ships', threatened in Yedo Bay in 1854 and later demonstrated at Kagoshima and Shimonoseki, was an intolerable humiliation to men who, although they had done no fighting for over two hundred years, were reckoned as professional soldiers and were marked out from the common people by the cherished right of wearing two swords. The idea of reviving national power provided the dominant motive for the movement of reform; for this end no obstruction was too great to be overcome and no institution too venerable to escape abolition or alteration—except only the Imperial monarchy itself, the most ancient and venerable of all, which was made the rallying-point of the whole reformation.

During the first few years after Perry's ultimatum the outraged patriotism of the *samurai* expressed itself in the cry 'Expel the barbarians!' The Shogunate was blamed for unpreparedness and cowardice, and it was thought that the purchase of a few guns of up-to-date type for coast defence would enable

Japan to defy the foreign fleets and regain her right to
seclusion. But after the powerful batteries installed
by the Choshu clansmen to command the Straits of
Shimonoseki had been destroyed by the expedition
of the allied Western powers, it became clear to all
but a remnant of conservatives that Japan could only
save herself from impotence and subjection by throwing open her gates even more widely than they had
been forced open and by learning all that the
foreigner had to teach. Already two young men of
Choshu had 'run away to sea' (rendering themselves
liable to a capital penalty under the old law which
forbade Japanese to go abroad) and worked their
passage to England before the mast. Their names
were Ito and Inouye.

The exposure of the state's weakness and inefficiency in the face of foreign aggression caused a widespread restlessness and discontent among the *samurai*,
many of whom were already dissatisfied with the
existing order of things on economic grounds. Great
numbers of the *samurai* were hopelessly burdened
with debt from which they had no escape. They
were forbidden to engage in trade and their fixed
salaries were payable in rice—a fact which turned
to their disadvantage with the growth of money
economy and speculative dealing which went on
during the Tokugawa period. Even more poverty-
stricken and ready for change were the *rōnin* or 'wave
men'—*samurai* who had left, or been dismissed from,
the service of their lords, and therefore had no

regular means of subsistence, but still regarded themselves as belonging to the military noble caste. There was thus a revolutionary situation within the ranks of the upper social class, and the unrest found its natural leaders in the local governments of the 'outside' clans. As against these forces of insurrection there were the vested interests of the clans which controlled the Yedo bureaucracy. The Tokugawa quasi-monarchy could not be expected to initiate radical reforms, since all the vested interests of the old régime centred upon it, and it was clear that if rapid progress was to be made, it must be overthrown. The 'outside' clans were only too willing to undertake the task. But Satsuma was believed to aspire to the Shogunate, and Choshu was as jealous of Satsuma as it was hostile to the house of Tokugawa. There was a great danger, therefore, that a successful revolt against the Tokugawa would only plunge the country into a period of confusion and civil strife, which would render it weaker than ever and invite foreign intervention or encroachments.

The revolution was saved from such an interregnum and breakdown of recognized authority by taking its leadership from the source that alone was able to give it full legitimacy—the Imperial dynasty. That this was possible was due to the fact that the Imperial dynasty, excluded for a thousand years from the exercise of real power, was itself a revolutionary force. With an origin in a prehistoric age and the sanction of the old national religion for its inalienable sovereignty, the line of the Mikados had persisted as the *de jure* monarchy while effective power had been usurped by one family after another of the Emperors' subjects. The *de facto* ruler had never dared to cut short the sacred line of descent from the Sun-goddess or to deny its right to reign. He had always found it more expedient politically to hold the person of the Emperor in virtual captivity and to legitimize his rule by extorting from his prisoner an administrative mandate with a suitable title of rank. The title of *shogun* (in full, *sei-i-tai-shogun* or 'barbarian-repressing commander-in-chief') was used by the Minamoto, Ashikaga, and Tokugawa dynasties of quasi-monarchs to give official style to their authority; it was not the only title which had been used in Japan for this purpose, but it is the one familiar to Western ears because it was borne by the Tokugawa. In course of time it had come to be accepted as a matter of constitutional theory that the Emperor reigned but did not govern. In the eighteenth century, however, a revival of the Shinto religion connected with the study of the *Kojiki*, the book which preserves the primitive Japanese mythology, led to a propagation of the doctrine, welcome in some quarters, that all power rightfully belonged to the Emperor and that the Shogun was nothing more than a minister who could be dismissed at will. There was therefore a chance for a revival of the Imperial power if ever the

Tokugawa should cease to be able to enforce the authority which they had won by the sword, and this was what happened after 1853. When Perry presented his demands, the *Shogun*'s government, which had its seat at Yedo (now Tokyo), pleaded that it could not give a reply before consulting the Emperor at Kyoto. The plea was made, partly to gain time, and partly because the *Shogun*'s government did not dare to accept the full responsibility for making the concessions it could not avoid. Whatever the motive, however, the result was disastrous for the Shogunate. The Imperial Court, consulted for the first time in generations on a matter of high policy began to take a line of its own, and quickly assumed the leadership of the forces of discontent which rallied to the slogan *son-o jo-i*, 'Revere the Emperor and expel the barbarians'. At first it assumed an ultra-conservative, anti-foreign attitude and rebuked the Shogunate for cowardice. Its order for the 'expulsion of the barbarians', and the heroic folly of the Choshu clan in attempting to carry it out by closing the Straits of Shimonoseki to foreign shipping, won more approval than did the inglorious prudence of the Yedo government, though the latter's refusal to obey the Imperial command saved Japan from any worse evil than the three-million-dollar indemnity exacted after the fighting at Shimonoseki. The demonstration by the foreign squadrons in Osaka Bay in 1865 convinced the Imperial Court that the barbarian-expelling policy was unwise, and no more was heard

H

of it, but it had served to discredit the Shogunate, which was now defied by Choshu and other clans, and was no longer able to control the activities of the Emperor and his entourage. Finally the fifteenth Tokugawa Shogun, Yoshinobu, was induced to resign his office and restore his administrative power to the Throne. The Shogunate was thereupon abolished and replaced by a provisional government of ministers appointed by the Emperor. The formerly privileged vassals of the Tokugawa family were excluded from the new government, and when they attempted a counter-revolution they were denounced as rebels and suppressed by forces drawn mainly from the 'outside' clans and acting in the name of the Emperor. The revolution was completed when the abolition of the Shogunate was followed in the next few years by the abolition of the feudal system; the feudal lords were persuaded to retire into private life with compensation for the loss of their revenues, and their retinues were disbanded, most of the *samurai* being absorbed into the service of the new centralized state, either into the civil administration or into the army, navy, and police forces.

The Japanese revolution of '68 was made by relatively unprivileged sections of the Japanese upper class—by the Kyoto Court nobles and the *samurai* of the 'outside' clans, and it was led by very young men in both these classes. Its rapid success and thoroughness of achievement were due to the fact that it was at one and the same time a revolution and a traditionalist restoration. It turned the flank of conservatism by appealing to a past more remote than the origins of the *ancien régime* which it attacked, and it engaged in a radical reform of institutions with the full support of the legitimate monarchy. The Imperial Court allied itself with the reformers because it had nothing to lose and much to gain by the destruction of the existing order. It was in no way bound up with the vested interests of the Yedo bureaucracy and the feudal magnates. The Emperor known to history by his reign title of Meiji came to the throne at the age of fifteen in 1867, received the executive power restored by the Shogun in the same year, and died in 1911 after seeing his country victorious in a war against one of the Great Powers of Europe.

China could expect no similar lead from the Court of Peking, which remained a stronghold of corrupt officialdom and obscurantist reaction while Japan was forging ahead year by year in the adoption of Western models, political and economic, on the initiative of the Emperor's government. The Chinese monarchy was identified with reactionary vested interests, and in this respect its position was similar to that of other oriental monarchies which governed as well as reigned and were therefore surrounded by courtiers and place-men with every reason to fear changes in the existing order. The fact that the Ch'ing dynasty was of alien (Manchu) origin was a further factor in making its policy ultra-conservative. It had long since ceased to depend on the might of Manchu arms to hold down the Chinese and relied on a rigid adherence to Confucian orthodoxy to win the support of the scholar class, so that it feared to take any initiative which might arouse hostility among the *literati*. Another consideration which counted for much with the Ch'ing Court was the tradition of opposition to the Manchus in the southern provinces, which had in the seventeenth century held out desperately against the conquerors long after the northern provinces had submitted, and were permanently dissatisfied with the quota of offices allotted to them in the civil service. As the principal contact with foreigners had been through the south coast ports, foreign influences and the desire for westernizing reforms first made their appearance in that quarter and came to be associated in the minds of the Manchu courtiers with the provinces that had always been the least loyal to the dynasty.

Fitzgerald[1] holds the view that the T'ai P'ing movement, had it not been crushed by the intervention of the Western powers, 'would, there is good reason to suppose, have done for China what the almost contemporary Meiji restoration movement did for Japan'. But this author seems to ignore the fundamental difference between the Meiji restoration with its appeal to the oldest national tradition, and its revival of the indigenous ancient religion of the

[1] Fitzgerald, op. cit., pp. 547 and 567–79.

country, and a movement drawing its main inspiration from a recently imported foreign faith. Mr. Fitzgerald has to admit that the identification of the T'ai P'ing rebellion with a persecuting Christianity was the great obstacle to its success, and it is hard to believe his contention that the new dynasty 'had every prospect of ultimate victory', if it had not been for the foreign intervention. The T'ai P'ing partisans were energetic and ruthless, but they set in opposition to themselves all the forces of conservatism; they could make no appeal to tradition and their domination remained precarious even in the provinces they overran. They failed to make any impression on the northern provinces. The triumph of the T'ai P'ing would have involved a radical religious and cultural revolution, and it is extremely improbable that opposition could have been so completely overcome as to have allowed the formation of a unified, stable government for the whole of China. A T'ai P'ing victory could not have had the double traditionalist-revolutionary character of the Meiji restoration. In China modernism could not be affiliated to tradition; it had to take the path of iconoclastic revolt. The insurgents' creed in the eighteen-fifties was politically monarchical, but it was Christian. In 1911 it was no longer Christian, but it was republican.

IV

THE EUROPEAN EMPIRES

BETWEEN 1840 and 1894 three of the Great
Powers of Europe acquired in full sovereignty
colonial possessions on, or close to, the shore of the
mainland of Asia between the Gulf of Siam and the
Sea of Okhotsk. England acquired the island of
Hong Kong and a fragment of the mainland opposite, France obtained the territories now unified
under the title of French Indo-China, and Russia
incorporated in her empire the region which to-day
forms the Far Eastern Area of the Soviet Union.
All these territorial gains were made at the expense
of China or her dependencies—with the exception
of the island of Sakhalin which Russia occupied in
defiance of a Japanese claim to sovereignty. The
lands annexed served their owners as bases of power
and were at the same time stakes of interest that involved them more closely in the affairs of the Far
East than purely commercial connexions could have
done. As a result of their holdings England, France,
and Russia were the established 'China Powers' in
1894. In that and the following years the Far
Eastern situation was radically transformed, first by
the rise of Japan as an active and no longer a passive factor in international relations, and secondly by
the enterprises of Germany and the U.S.A. But the
colonial domains of the earlier 'Big Three' were not

affected and have remained unreduced to the present day.

The colonial gain of England in the Far East was not comparable in extent to the acquisitions of France and Russia, but it rivalled them in importance. The seizure and annexation of Hong Kong provided the third term in the series of which India and Malaya were the first two. With this key stronghold on the coastline of southern China the arm of British imperial power reached most effectively to the Far East and gave a more than adequate political protection to a commerce that economically was well able to take care of itself against all competitors. The occupation of Hong Kong was recommended by Lord Napier in 1834 as calculated to provide a *point d'appui* for applying pressure to China, and it was actually carried out in 1839, when the island was used both as an asylum for the British traders evacuated from Canton and as a base for naval operations. It was decided to retain the island, not only to serve the same purposes in case of another conflict with China, but also to meet requirements which even with the new treaty provisions could not be satisfied in Canton: to obtain a site for a dock for refitting ships, bonded warehouses for the China trade, and a holiday resort under British administration for the Canton traders and their families. Its own commercial possibilities as a port were at first hardly realized; it contained no town at the time of its cession and only a scanty population of peasants

and fishermen. But within a few years it had become a great commercial centre. From the first it
was, like Singapore, a free port, open to the traders
of all nations on equal terms. It had an administration devoted to the encouragement of enterprises
auxiliary to trade, and it had the advantage of a
geographical position favoured by the new conditions of economic life in the Far East.

Under the old Chinese system of artificially re-
stricting foreign trade to a single port Canton had
been the terminus for European ships sailing to
China, but by the middle of the nineteenth century
its position had been modified in two ways. In the
first place, it was no longer the terminus after the
opening of the ports farther north, and its situation
at the head of an estuary left it out of the way for
shipping that went right up the coast to Shanghai.
And further, the Canton estuary was too shallow for
deep-draught shipping, so that with the development
in size of ocean-going vessels the city was placed
more and more at a disadvantage as a port. It remained the economic centre of the densely peopled
Si-kiang delta and the outlet for the trade of Kwangtung and Kwangsi provinces, but Hong Kong became the port of call for the high seas traffic and
the deep-water port for Canton. Goods both from
Europe or America and from other parts of the Far
East were transhipped there and loaded on small
steamers to be sent up the river. It also became the
distributing centre for the lesser ports of Kwangtung

and Fukien, and later on added certain manufactur-
ing industries to its ever-expanding commerce.

The island of Hong Kong itself has an area of
only 32 square miles, but the present colony of
Greater Hong Kong covers nearly 400 ; the enlarge-
ment has been made by the addition of the Kowloon
peninsula on the opposite side of Victoria harbour
in 1860, the cession being exacted after the Second
Anglo-Chinese war, and by the acquisition of a
further tract of mainland and small islands on a 99-
years lease in 1898. Both extensions were made
primarily for strategic reasons, to render the island
and harbour defensible against attack either from
the Chinese mainland or from a hostile navy. The
article of cession in the treaty of 1860 declared Kowloon to be handed over for 'the maintenance of law
and order in and about the Harbour of Hong Kong'.
The acquisition of the so-called New Territories on
lease in 1898 was part of the 'Battle of the Concessions' of that year, and expressed the alarm of the
British Government at the drive of other Powers for
leased territories and spheres of influence in China,
beginning with the German seizure of Kiaochow in
the previous year.

The possession of Hong Kong certainly gave to
England a preponderance of prestige as against other
Western Powers in dealing with China. As long as
the Court of Peking, ill informed about the affairs
of the outer world, made and applied treaties in its
foreign relations only as a concession to superior

I

force, the nation which had its power visibly established near at hand enjoyed an immense advantage for diplomacy. Hong Kong not only commanded the approach to Canton, but was nearer than the territorial base of any other Western Power to the ports of central and northern China. It naturally became the objective of British policy to prevent the acquisition by any other Western Power of a base nearer than Hong Kong to the Yangtse delta or the Tientsin–Peking region; in other words, to keep closed against the territorial aggrandisement, though not against the commercial competition, of other Western Powers all the coastline of Asia between Hong Kong and the Japan Sea. England did not seek a monopolist ascendancy in China, and pursued a free-trade policy even in Hong Kong, but the very cause of free trade itself required a superiority of power sufficient to prevent the formation of spheres of exclusive privilege. Free trade, as championed by England in the nineteenth century, was the cause of the stronger in purely commercial competition. The 'sphere of influence' with its special rights was the objective of states which sought to compensate for weakness in such competition by the direct application of political power. With a free-trade policy England in 1894 took two-thirds of the total foreign trade of China, and her diplomacy was by that time directed not so much to extracting new treaty rights from China as to maintaining and strengthening the Chinese central government in its rule over its vast empire. England stood to gain more from the 'open door' to the whole Chinese empire than from any partition. Some other Powers, however, were disposed to regard with a more hopeful eye the symptoms of a coming break-up of the loosely knit realm.

England's two rivals in colonial acquisition in the Far East between 1840 and 1894 were France and Russia, the one approaching China from the south and the other from the north. Russia in 1840 already possessed a belt of territory right across northern Asia to the Okhotsk Sea and the Bering Strait, but the whole basin of the Amur was recognized as belonging to China, and the frontier in that quarter had not been altered since 1689. France had as yet no territorial foothold in the Far East, but a special connexion with Annam dating from the eighteenth century. When Hong Kong was ceded to England there was no other European stronghold on the coast of Asia between Singapore and the Okhotsk Sea, and this was the state of affairs until 1854 when Russia was stirred to activity in the Far East by the consequences of the Crimean war.

The original advance of the Russians across Siberia had brought them to the Okhotsk Sea in 1639, five years before the Manchus seized Peking and set up the Ch'ing dynasty in China. The Manchu kingdom, expanding from what is now central Manchuria, had made conquests to the north as well as to the south, and the new Manchu–Chinese empire claimed control over both banks of the Amur river. The

attempt of the Russians to force their way down the
Amur and make the river their highway of communication from the region of Lake Baikal to the
Pacific met with vigorous opposition from the Manchus—an opposition which the Russians in the seventeenth century were quite unable to overcome. They
were forced to admit defeat and to accept a frontier
along the divide of the Stanovoi mountains to the
north of the Amur, with no right of navigation on
the river. This arrangement was maintained for
more than a century and a half, Russia's quiescence
being due partly to lack of effective power in a
region so remote, partly to preoccupations elsewhere,
and partly to lack of a strong economic motive for
a fresh advance. The Amur route was not necessary
for the trade between Russia and China, which was
carried on by caravan across Mongolia, so that
Kiakhta south of Lake Baikal was virtually the terminus of the overland road to the east from European
Russia. The Okhotsk littoral, on the other hand,
and the settlements in Kamchatka, the Aleutian
Islands, and Alaska, which subsisted mainly on the
seal and sea-otter fur trade, were reached more easily
by sea than by land from Russia, so that there was
no pressing need for development of a west–east
line of communication beyond Lake Baikal. But by
the middle of the nineteenth century the Russians
were showing a new activity in the Amur region,
sending expeditions for trade and exploration into
Chinese territory and taking advantage of the de-

cline of the central power in Peking to obtain a hold
on an area of country which was very sparsely inhabited and lightly administered. Even without the
Crimean war there would probably have been an
extension of the Russian empire to the Amur and
beyond during the fifties and sixties. As it was, the
crisis in the affairs of Europe reacted on Russo-
Chinese relations by giving Russia a strong incentive
and pretext for violent action. Lacking command of
the sea, Russia was cut off from communication with
the Far East by maritime routes, and Petropavlovsk
in Kamchatka, which was at that time the chief
base of Russian shipping and naval power in the
Pacific, was threatened with an Anglo-French attack.
For the succour of their exposed Pacific coastline
the Russians demanded from China in 1854 a right
of way down the Amur, and enforced their demand
with a strong flotilla which descended the river to
its mouth. China, distracted by the T'ai P'ing rebellion—the insurgents had captured Nanking in
the previous year—was unable to offer any resistance,
and the Russians in effect held the whole line of the
Amur, cutting off all the territory to the north of
the river. The military need which had prompted
the move ceased to be imperative after the close of
the Crimean war, but possession persuaded to an
assertion of sovereignty, the more so as the Russian
Tsardom, humiliated and frustrated in its Near
Eastern policy, craved an easy success in some other
field of foreign affairs to restore its prestige and self-

confidence. Thus the only gain Russia had to show for a three-years war against Turkey, England, France, and Sardinia was the seizure of a couple of hundred thousand square miles of Chinese territory, China having had no connexion whatever with the conflict out of which the Crimean war began.

The Russians found it easy to occupy territory in the north-eastern corner of the Chinese empire when Peking was busy with the T'ai P'ing rebels and, after 1856, with a war against England and France. The difficulty was rather to obtain formal recognition of the conquest from China without applying coercion to the weakened, but still proud, empire through its vital nerve-centres far to the south. Russia was not well placed for such action and, if she were to attempt it, ran the risk of renewing the hostility of England and France. She gained her end, however, not by direct extortion, but rather as a price for assistance in a situation which confronted China with a choice of evils. In 1858 Russia appeared in the rôle of a highly paid counsel on behalf of China, a rôle which she was to play in an even more striking manner in 1895. Russia offered herself as mediator between a defeated China and England and France, and thus rendered a service to the Peking Court, which was infinitely more alarmed by the Anglo-French occupation of Canton and the threat to the capital than by the Russian encroachments in Manchuria. In consideration of her diplomatic aid Russia was allowed to annex all the territory north of the Amur which belonged to China by virtue of the Russo-Chinese treaty of 1689, and the littoral to the south of the lower Amur as far as the border of Korea and inland to the Ussuri was placed under joint Russian and Chinese control—a transitional arrangement leading to outright cession to Russia two years later (1860).

The Russians now held the Pacific coastline of Asia from the Bering Strait to Possiet Bay, and in 1875 they obtained from Japan recognition of their claim to the island of Sakhalin. Japan at the beginning of the nineteenth century had no clearly defined northern boundary. There was no organized administration north of Yezo[1] (which was itself a colony rather than an integral part of Japan), but Japanese traders and fishermen frequented the shores of Sakhalin and the Kurile Islands, and the aboriginal inhabitants (Ainu, Gilyak, and Kamchadal) were too few and scattered to count politically, so that Japan met Russian penetration in this area with a claim to ownership. Russia held Kamchatka from the time of Peter the Great, and Russians and Japanese came into contact in the Kuriles. The idea of opening up trade with Japan from Kamchatka was mooted in St. Petersburg as early as 1791, but all attempts in this direction were abortive, and in 1806 the

---

[1] Yezo, the most northerly of the four large islands of Japan, is now generally known under the designation of Hokkaidō or 'north-sea district', but this name covers the Kuriles (Chishima) as well as Yezo itself.

Russians, having no motive for maintaining good
relations with Japan, began to indulge in piratical
raids on Japanese settlements and shipping as far
south as Yezo. Negotiations subsequently took place
which led to a division of the Kuriles in 1814, the
Russians taking the islands north of Urup and the
Japanese those to the south of it. Urup itself was
left as a neutral zone, and nothing was said about
Sakhalin.

There was no further development in the situation
until the fifties, when Russia's occupation of the
mainland littoral of the Gulf of Tartary gave a new
importance to Sakhalin. In 1859 Count Muraviev,
Governor-General of East Siberia, who had been the
inspiration of the forward policy on the Amur, sailed
to Yokohama with a squadron of seven ships and
demanded the cession of Sakhalin, but he found the
Japanese in no mood to yield and left without
achieving his purpose. During the next few years
desultory negotiations took place and both Russian
and Japanese settlers established themselves in the
island; the harsh climatic conditions were more
favourable to the former than to the latter, and
Russian local authorities continually encroached on
the Japanese. The Japanese Government, preoccupied after 1868 with the task of national reconstruction and reluctant to risk a major crisis in foreign
affairs for the sake of a barren and frigid territory,
finally decided to abandon all claims to Sakhalin in
return for a corresponding renunciation by Russia

with regard to the Kuriles. A treaty was concluded
on these terms in 1875. Russia was induced to agree
to this solution by the course of events in the Balkans,
which led her for the time being to close her account
in the Far East.

Russia's Far Eastern expansion in the period 1850–
75 was the product of two different types of colonial
activity—a west-to-east land-power advance from
Lake Baikal and a north-to-south sea-power advance
along the coast from Kamchatka and the Okhotsk
Sea. The territories gained by these two lines of
movement formed a continuous area, but not a com-
pact whole, for the Primorsk or Maritime Province
reached nearly twelve degrees of latitude farther
south on the Japan Sea coast than the Russo-Chinese
boundary on the middle Amur. Its natural hinterland, therefore, was not Russian Siberia but Chinese
Manchuria, and it was essentially an 'overseas' rather
than an 'overland' colony. Nevertheless, the partial
isolation of the Primorsk by the huge salient of
northern Manchuria was not a really important fact
of political geography until the last decade of the
century, because the whole of the Pacific littoral of
Siberia was nearer to Russia by sea than by land as
long as transport across Siberia was only by pack-
horse and tarantass. Only with the building of the
Trans-Siberian railway did overland communications with the Far East come to be of primary importance, and then the desire to carry the line by the
shortest route to the most southerly of the Russian

K

Pacific ports, i.e. Vladivostok, led to the scheme for cutting through Manchuria with all its momentous political implications.

The Russians failed to obtain a straighter frontier for East Siberia during this period, partly because their sea-power, so effective for the advance down the coast, could not be brought to bear in the interior, and partly because Manchuria was more valuable to China than the Primorsk territory and there was in Peking a stronger resolve to defend it. Quite apart from the traditional associations of the Manchu dynasty with the Kirin district from which its power had first been derived, inland Manchuria was, and is, naturally a far more favoured region than the littorals of the Japan Sea and Gulf of Tartary in the same degrees of latitude a little way to the east. Both Manchuria and the Primorsk suffer, along with the whole of Northern Asia, from intensely cold winters, but whereas Manchuria has a hot and relatively dry summer well suited to agriculture, the Primorsk is afflicted by a very wet, chilly summer, due to prevailing onshore winds from a sea which is chilled by a cold current descending from the Arctic. It had never, before the arrival of the Russians, been colonized by Chinese, Koreans, or Japanese, nor had it been the home of warlike, tribally organized barbarians such as the Mongols and Manchus. It was uninhabited save for a very scanty population of aboriginal hunters and fishermen. China, beset with evils from domestic and foreign conflicts, hardly felt the loss of this wilderness land which she ceded to Russia in 1860. But Manchuria was another matter, and the Chinese made it clear that they would resist any attempt of the Russians to advance south of the Amur or west of the Ussuri.

For the Russians the Primorsk was of value not so much for its own sake, but rather as a stepping-stone to the south. The new port of Vladivostok, founded in 1860 on the desolate shore of Peter the Great Bay, was a great advance on any base the Russians had previously possessed. It was only about two hundred miles farther away by sea from Shanghai than the British territorial base at Hong Kong. But Vladivostok was not yet out of range of winter sea-ice, and to obtain an ice-free port it was necessary to continue the advance still farther south. On a coast or island between the Japan and the East China Sea Russia might defy the winter and at the same time establish a stronghold nearer than Hong Kong to the ports of central and northern China, gaining a corresponding ascendancy in the affairs of the Far East.

The first attempt was made in 1861, when the Russian corvette *Possadnik* arrived off the Japanese island of Tsushima in the straits of that name between Japan and Korea, and on the pretext that she was in need of repairs proceeded to set up a naval depot there. In reply to anxious inquiries from Yedo the Russians explained that they had come to forestall the English, who had designs on the island, and suggested that they should be allowed to stay. The *Shogun*'s government, however, appealed to England against the Russian action, and a British naval unit visited Tsushima, where it found the Russian flag flying. Vigorous representations both to the Russian local authorities and to St. Petersburg resulted in the withdrawal of the Russian pioneer force on Tsushima, honour being saved by the pretence that there had never been any intention of making a permanent settlement there. This was the first move of a policy which was ultimately to lead to the alignment of England and Japan against Russia in the Far East and to the Russo-Japanese war. The Tsushima episode of 1861 had no serious repercussions at the time, but it foreshadowed the later and more serious Russian attempt to attain the same objective through the control of Korea.

There was no further extension of the Russian empire in full sovereignty on the Far Eastern mainland after 1860, and the frontiers then established are to-day those of the Soviet Union. The territory acquired from China in the fifties was, as has been pointed out, very sparsely inhabited, and even with a small influx of Russian colonists it soon became more thoroughly Russian than other parts of East Siberia where the aboriginal population was more numerous, so that in time the boundary came to be one of nationality and not simply a political frontier. The Russian people, and not merely the rule of the Tsar, was established in the Siberian Maritime Pro-

vince, and this fact is now more than ever of vital
importance for Far Eastern politics.

France was the third European Great Power to
acquire territory on the Pacific littoral of Asia during
the nineteenth century. The building of the French
colony of Indo-China began in 1862 with the annexation of part of Cochin-China and was completed
as a result of the Franco-Chinese war of 1883–5.
The French expansion was not directly at the expense of China, but involved the subjection of China's
tributary or vassal kingdom of Annam and thus led
ultimately to war against the suzerain Power. The
Annamese kingdom was a loose-knit realm, consisting
of the two rich deltaic plains of the Songkoi or Red
River (Tongking) and the Mekong (Cochin-China)
linked together by a long, narrow strip of mountain-
backed coastal plain (Annam proper). The Annamese originally came from Tongking, which was
conquered by the Chinese at the end of the third
century B.C. and was intermittently under Chinese
control for a thousand years. Even after throwing
off the Chinese yoke in the tenth century A.D. and
themselves entering on a career of conquest towards
the south, the Annamese retained a culture essentially Chinese in type—a characteristic separating
them from their southern neighbours, the Khmers
(Cambodians) and the Chams, whose cultural pattern was Indian. The Annamese in the end completely subdued the Chams (who held the modern
Cochin-China and southern Annam) and disputed

with Siam for ascendancy over the once powerful kingdom of Cambodia, which had its centre in the plain round Lake Tonlé Sap to the north-west of Cochin-China. In the eighteenth century the Annamese 'empire' had its capital at Hué, residence of a suzerain king who in his turn paid tribute to China, while Tongking and Cochin-China were ruled by virtually independent feudatory princes. The Cochin-China vassal dynasty was threatened towards the end of the century by a revolt, and in 1787 the reigning prince sought the aid of France, concluding a treaty with Louis XVI through the agency of the French missionary Pigneau de Behaine, Bishop of Adran. France, foiled in her Indian empire-building by the English, saw an opportunity for compensatory gains farther east. The outbreak of the French Revolution and the wars that ensued prevented France from reaping the benefits of the treaty, but a number of French officers took service with the Cochin-China prince and enabled him not only to defeat his local enemies but also to become king of Annam in 1801. The Catholic Church, meanwhile, protected as a condition of the military aid, gained many converts and became an object of suspicion to the new royal dynasty. An era of persecution began after 1830, and French and Spanish priests as well as Annamese converts were put to death.

The tradition of French influence and the plight of the Catholic Church in Annam gave an opportunity for action to the French Second Empire.

Napoleon III was anxious for reasons of domestic politics to pose as protector of the Church, and in his
friendship with England, confirmed by the alliance
in the Crimean war, he had secured the condition
necessary for success in a Far Eastern venture. England was no longer in a mood to obstruct all French
expansion in the East, and was prepared to allow
France to acquire a new colonial possession, provided
that it was neither too close to India nor on the
farther side of Hong Kong. The French joined the
British in making war on China in 1857, and in
the following year also invaded Annam in company
with a Spanish force from the Philippines. After
the conclusion of the war with China the French
pursued the Annam campaign more vigorously, and
by a treaty in 1862 obtained the cession of the
three eastern provinces of Cochin-China. From this
base the French gradually extended their control,
gaining a protectorate over Cambodia in 1863, annexing the western provinces of Cochin-China in
1867, and imposing a protectorate on Annam itself
in 1874. The king of Annam undertook to 'conform
his policy to that of France', but secretly he appealed
to China, as a vassal of the Chinese empire, and
endeavoured to evade the terms of the treaty. When
in the early eighties the French Third Republic
began to pursue an active colonial policy—which in
the Far East took the form of an expedition to Tongking—China asserted her right as suzerain over
Annam. This led to hostilities between France and

China, in the course of which the Chinese were ultimately defeated—though not before they had inflicted serious reverses on the French colonial forces in Tongking. By the Franco-Chinese treaty of 1885 China renounced all claim to interfere in the affairs of Annam and recognized the French protectorate. In 1887 Cochin-China, Cambodia, Annam proper and Tongking were grouped together as French Indo-China under a Governor-General, and the Laos tribal territory to the north of Cambodia was added as a fifth province in 1893.

The Franco-Chinese war of 1883–5 brought about a certain tension between France and England, whose relations were already strained over the question of the British occupation of Egypt. The British regarded with suspicion the French naval operations on the south coast of China and occupation of the Pescadores Islands in the Formosa Strait, fearing the establishment of a permanent French base somewhere between Hong Kong and Shanghai. They were still more alarmed when in 1885 King Thibaw of Burma entered into close relations with the French administration in Tongking and began to pursue an anti-British policy. The First and Second Burmese wars had already placed the maritime provinces of Arakan, Pegu and Tenasserim under British rule ; the rest of Burma had the status formerly possessed by Annam—that is to say, it was virtually independent, but paid tribute to China. The prospect of a French overland penetration of Burma and approach to India was too much for the Viceroy of India, Lord Dufferin, who made war on Thibaw, captured and deported him to India, and annexed his country. China, after her experience in the case of Annam, made no attempt to protect her vassal, but the tribute payment due from Burma continued to be remitted to Peking until 1900.

Of the three large states between the Bay of Bengal and the South China Sea, one was thus annexed by France, one by England, and one remained sovereign. Siam, situated between Annam and Burma, retained her independence, not so much on account of a strength lacking in the other two kingdoms, as because of the need of two rival imperialist Powers for a buffer state and the difficulty of making partition of a country with such an emphatic geographical and national unity. Even so, the integrity of Siam was in jeopardy and an acute Anglo-French conflict was nearly precipitated in 1893, when hostilities occurred between French and Siamese outposts on a disputed boundary and a French flotilla blockaded Bangkok. Demands for the cession of nearly a third of the territory of Siam were made by the French, and Siam would probably have yielded but for the presence of British warships which had been sent to watch the situation at the Siamese capital. As it was, Siam escaped with a comparatively small loss of territory and the payment of an indemnity. As a sequel to the incident England and France entered into negotiations, and in 1896 concluded a convention by which both Powers guaranteed the independence of Siam with a reservation of non-contiguous spheres of influence for themselves.

V

THE RAILWAY ACROSS ASIA

AS early as 1885 Russia planned the building of a
railway which should traverse Asia from west
to east and link her European homeland with the
most southerly of her ports on the Pacific, the twenty-
five-year-old town of Vladivostok. The line was to
follow the old Siberian road to Irkutsk, thence to go
round the southern end of Lake Baikal and run east
again with a detour far to the north, avoiding the
salient of northern Manchuria, until it reached Khabarovsk at the junction of the Ussuri and the Amur;
thence almost due south to Vladivostok. The Vladivostok–Khabarovsk section was taken in hand in
1891, work was started on other sections in the
following year, and by 1895 the line was completed
from the Urals to Lake Baikal.

The building of the Trans-Siberian railway was
a political event of the greatest importance. It pro-
foundly affected the relations of the Great Powers of
Europe. In the first place, it enabled Russia to escape
as regards her Far Eastern policy from the ultimate
domination to which she, along with the other European Continental Powers, was subjected by reason
of England's paramount sea-power. From the year
of the battle of Trafalgar the naval supremacy of
England in the eastern Atlantic and Mediterranean
was not seriously challenged, and it was the ultimate

arbiter in conflicts arising out of the overseas colonial policies of the other European nations. Russia alone, having direct entry into Asia by land, had the capacity for evading this supremacy, but until the building of the Trans-Siberian railway her advantage was merely potential. Siberia was so thinly peopled, distances so great and the means of transport so wretched that it was not possible for Russia to concentrate and supply a large army east of the Urals. Her Far Eastern conquests in the fifties were made, as we have seen, at the expense of a China weakened by internal revolt and foreign war, and did not require any great military strength. Russia was in fact incapable at that time of pressing even China really hard, as was shown by her acceptance of the Amur boundary line with its awkward salient separating Transbaikalia from the Primorsk and by her climb-down over the Ili boundary dispute in 1881, when a reunited China showed a disposition to resort to force. Russia's primary means of communication with her Far Eastern territories were by sea, and in so far as she was dependent on maritime transport she was subject to English sea-power just as much as France or Germany. This situation was altered when the vast spaces of Russia-in-Asia began to be contracted by railways. First the Trans-Caspian, which skirted the frontier of Persia and filled British statesmen with 'mervousness' for the safety of the Indian empire, and then the Trans-Siberian, which aimed at the shore of the Pacific in close proximity to China, Korea and Japan.

In both these directions Russia threatened the established imperial interests of England. In India England held sovereignty, in China a diplomatic and commercial preponderance, and in both cases her ascendancy was based in the last analysis on sea-power. By her command of the sea she had controlled and restricted the activities of her European rivals, and she had needed only small land forces for dealing with her Asiatic opponents. But now that she was confronted in Asia with the military power of Russia based on overland railways, against which sea-power was of no avail, the problem of imperial strategy appeared in a different guise.

The danger was first apprehended with regard to India, and was in that quarter very much exaggerated, for India was provided with incomparable natural ramparts in the great mountain barrier which enveloped her on the landward side, and it was not hard to keep the Russians on the other side of the Hindu Kush. The Chinese empire afforded a far more alluring prospect to Russian ambition. It lay open to the north with no high mountains east of the Altai and with the Gobi desert stopping short of Manchuria, the seat of its monarchy was situated in the extreme north of China proper, and the British had no territorial base north of Hong Kong. In these circumstances the idea of a Russian hegemony in the Far East, which fascinated Russian soldiers and politicians at the close of the century, was by no means so fantastic as it has appeared to be since the historical verdict of the Russo-Japanese war. The defeat of the Russian design was the result of the Anglo-Japanese Alliance, and the issue depended on the military efficiency of the Japanese. England by herself could never have taken Port Arthur, and if Japan had not proved an exception to the rule of oriental backwardness in military competence, there was no factor in the situation likely to frustrate a Russian conquest of Manchuria and Korea. The rise of Japan as a powerful modernized state, capable of taking the offensive, was a development contrary to all experience, a caprice of destiny deranging calculations which assumed as beyond question the principle that all politics in Asia and Africa were 'colonial' with 'native' states as passive, and not active, factors in the making of history. General Dragomirov was speaking correctly by the accepted political doctrine of his day when he dismissed the danger to the Russian position from Japan with the remark that 'Far Eastern affairs are decided in Europe', meaning that as long as no Great Power in Europe was ranged with England against Russia, there was no need to fear England's alliance with an Asiatic state.

As regards her diplomatic relations in Europe, Russia's position was indeed a strong one from the time she turned the spear-point of her ambition away from Europe into Asia. The concentration of Russian power on Far Eastern objectives meant a relaxation of the Austro-Russian rivalry in the Balkans which, in consequence of the Austro-German alliance of 1879, involved also a Russo-German conflict. Austria and Germany were only too glad to see Russia transfer her attention from Bulgaria to China and were ready to give her every support and encouragement as long as her activity was confined to a region well away from the frontiers of Austria. France was equally interested in supporting Russia on account of the Franco-Russian alliance concluded in 1893, for France could only retain this alliance by giving full rein to Russian ambition. It was thus impossible for England to form an anti-Russian coalition in Europe on the Far Eastern Question as she had been able to do on the old Straits-and-Balkans Eastern Question. Neither Austria, Germany nor France had reason to oppose Russia on Far Eastern issues, and both France and Germany were prepared actively to co-operate with Russia in that part of the world for making colonial or semi-colonial gains at the expense of the established British ascendancy.

The building of the Trans-Siberian railway gave Russia the means to pursue a forward policy in the Far East, and at the same time the alliance with France provided her with security for her rear in case of a Far Eastern war. Thus the conclusion of the alliance led directly to the diversion of Russian policy from Europe. This was certainly not foreseen or desired by the French promoters of the alliance, who thought in terms of European politics and hoped to put pressure on Germany by bringing together the two Powers with grievances against her. There were

two outstanding feuds in Europe, the one between
France and Germany on account of the unforgiven
annexation of Alsace-Lorraine and the other between
Russia and Austria over Balkan issues. These two
unrelated quarrels were linked together by the system of alliances. Had Austria allied herself with
France, Germany and Russia would have come together, but Austria was drawn into the orbit of
Germany, and after the publication of the Austro-
German treaty of alliance and the lapse of Bismarck's
'reinsurance' treaty with Russia, it was inevitable
that France and Russia should combine in opposition
to the Austro-German bloc. With the conclusion of
the Franco-Russian alliance in 1893 all the five continental Great Powers of Europe were in one or other
of the two groups. Italy adhered to the German side,
and England alone stood outside in 'splendid isolation'. A general war on the Continent appeared to
be imminent. But it was postponed for twenty years
because Russia, instead of pressing her quarrel with
Austria, turned away and gave herself up to the Far
Eastern adventure, which was only liquidated in
1905 after the disastrous war with Japan. In 1907
the Austro-Russian conflict broke out afresh and
involved Europe in one crisis after another until it
precipitated the general war of 1914.

Russia's departure from Europe in the nineties
was not in accordance with the interests of France,
which required that the Franco-Russian group should
exert its maximum strength in Europe. But France

could not restrain Russia without risking the loss of her alliance, for as long as Russia refrained from a policy menacing to Austria there was nothing to prevent a Russo-German *rapprochement*, if Russia did not receive adequate support from France. Germany was similarly anxious to keep Russia busy in Asia and relieve the tension in the Balkans. Apart from these motives, both France and Germany saw profit for themselves in combining with Russia to break down the British hegemony in the Far East. Thus was formed that loose coalition of France, Germany and Russia known as the East Asiatic Dreibund, which first showed itself in the diplomatic arena by intervention against Japan in 1895 and was still a reality ten years later. The Dreibund cut right across the lines of Dual and Triple Alliance in Europe, and was in fact a bloc of the continental Powers against England. The Dreibund was on paper a very formidable combination of Powers, and up to a point it was an effective working partnership. But it could not be a really solid instrument fit to take the strain of a great war, for whereas both France and Germany were friends of Russia, they continued to view each other with hostility and suspicion. There was never, therefore, a genuine united front against England, and, such as it was, the Dreibund ceased to exist after 1905, when the Russo-Japanese war was fought to a finish with England holding the ring, and a disappointed Russia turned back again from Asia into Europe.

M

The period of Russia's concentration on Far Eastern affairs lasted for just over ten years, beginning with the Triple Intervention against Japan in the spring of 1895, and ending with the Treaty of Portsmouth, which concluded the Russo-Japanese war in the autumn of 1905. The occasion for Russia's first move was supplied by the dispute and war between Japan and China over Korea. This war exposed China's real weakness and at the same time gave Russia an opportunity to assume the role of China's friend and protector. The appearance of a Japanese army on the mainland of Asia coincided in time with the completion of more than half of the Trans-Siberian railway, and indeed the two events were not unrelated, for the Japanese action in Korea in 1894 was inspired by a resolve to deal with China before Russia had finished her railway-building and developed her full strength in the Far East.

Twenty-six years had passed since the Meiji Restoration of 1868, and the group of reformers who then took charge of the government of Japan had carried through their programme and provided their country with the power-making apparatus of a modern state. They had built up an army and navy of European style, the former with German, and the latter with English, expert assistance. They had substituted an efficient centralized bureaucracy for the old feudal system, developed industries, and especially war material industries, with the direct aid of the state, and had promulgated a parliamentary consti-

tution which drew a considerable part of the nation
into active political life while leaving the executive
responsible only to the Emperor. In China, on the
other hand, the traditionalists had remained in control of the government, and the changes which had
been made to meet the urgent needs of national defence had been merely superficial. Ships and guns
had been purchased from abroad since the humiliation of 1860, and the fighting services to some extent
trained and equipped in a modern way, but there
was no such drive behind the reforms as there was
in Japan, and a British naval officer who served with
the Chinese fleet [1] speaks of 'the national machine of
organized inefficiency' which was pitted against Japan
in the war of 1894. Everything in the administration
was at the mercy of the ignorant and corrupt palace
eunuch Li Lien-ying, favourite of the Empress
Dowager, the fleet was placed under the command
of a cavalry officer, the Director of the Arsenal was,
it appears, in the pay of Japan, and even the Chihli
Viceroy, Li Hung-chang, who had created the new-
model fighting forces, contributed to their undoing,
for, in the words of the same author, 'the corruption,
peculation, and nepotism which infested his organizations had their fountain-head in himself, and to an
extent which was exceptional even for a Chinese
official'.

When war broke out, the twelve-inch guns of
China's two battleships were provided with just three

[1] W. F. Tyler, *Pulling Strings in China*, pp. 35 et seqq.

fighting shells, one for the flagship and two for her
sister. This fact was known to the Japanese navy,
but not to European observers, who were impressed
by the Chinese fleet's paper superiority in heavy guns,
and generally took the view that China had at least
an even chance of victory.

Since the Restoration Japan had been in conflict
with China over the status of the two intervening
kingdoms of Ryukyu and Korea. The king of the
Ryukyu Islands, a chain lying between Kyushu and
Formosa and inhabited by people speaking a dialect
of Japanese, paid tribute to China and also to the
Japanese lords of Satsuma. The king of Korea paid
tribute to China only. Both states were not only in
practice independent as regards their internal affairs,
but claimed the right to make treaties with foreign
Powers. China, however, as tribute-receiving suzerain, was held to have a right of general supervision
and occasional intervention. How far China actually
interfered with the policies of her vassal kingdoms
depended on her strength and energy at any particular time. This system of quasi-feudal relations
had been in keeping with the traditional order of
things in which the Western concept of state sovereignty had not been developed, but it could not
survive unchallenged in the new world of which
China and Japan were now a part. The two vassal
kingdoms had either to assume sovereignty or to be
definitely subjected to Chinese rule or to come under
the sway of Japan. The initial aim of Japanese policy

was to annex the Ryukyu Islands, making use of the old Satsuma supremacy there, and to make Korea into an independent buffer state, abolishing the Chinese suzerainty. The annexation of Ryukyu was accomplished without difficulty, and the islands were formally declared to be part of Japan in 1879. The task in Korea, on the other hand, proved to be by no means an easy one, for a powerful faction in Seoul opposed any Japanese intervention, and China made a vigorous effort to turn her suzerainty into a real domination.

Two motives dictated Japanese policy with regard to Korea. First and foremost was the fear, analogous to England's traditional fear for the Low Countries, lest Korea should fall under the control of some more powerful state and become the spear-head of an attack on Japan—a purpose which the peninsula had served in the time of Kublai Khan. Japan's security clearly depended on either a Japanese control of Korea or the maintenance there of a fully independent buffer state—for Korea by herself could never be strong enough to threaten Japan. Two greater Powers were contiguous with Korea on the mainland—China with her traditional rights of suzerainty, and Russia with her naval station of Vladivostok just north of the Korean border. It might seem that a Chinese suzerainty was no threat to Japan in view of the general weakness of China, but on a long view it was certainly dangerous, for either China would grow stronger through westernization and become a Great Power in reality or, alternatively, she was liable to fall under Russian domination as Russia's Far Eastern power increased —in which case China's suzerainty over Korea might be converted informally into a Russian protectorate. To get rid of the Chinese supremacy in Korea was therefore the primary aim of Japan's policy.

In addition to the security motive there was a strong economic urge to open up the Korean market. Since Japan had had foreign trade thrust upon her by the Western powers, she had herself acquired an enthusiasm for that commercial activity which a British consul in China [1] described as 'the true herald of civilization . . . the human agency appointed under a Divine dispensation to work out man's emancipation from the thraldom and evils of a savage isolation'. The Japanese in the seventies and eighties showed all the zeal of converts for the new religion and eagerly sought for markets on the Asiatic mainland. But in China they enjoyed neither extraterritorial rights, 'settlements' for residence nor most-favoured-nation treatment, and were therefore at a disadvantage for trade in comparison with nationals of the Western Powers. In Korea, on the other hand, Japan saw an opportunity to be first in the field. Korea had adhered to the seclusionist principle after both Japan and China had been forced to abandon

[1] Rutherford Alcock, article in the *Bombay Quarterly Review*, April 1856.

it and did not sign any treaty for foreign intercourse before 1876, thus earning for herself the title of 'the Hermit Kingdom'. When she did at last yield, it was not to a Western Power, but to Japan, who now broke into Korea's seclusion as America twenty-three years before had broken into her own. In the Kianghwa Treaty of 1876 Japan recognized Korea as an independent state enjoying 'the same sovereign rights as does Japan' (no mention being made of Korea's tributary relation to China) and exacted from her unilateral concessions on the model of those previously obtained by the Western Powers in China and Japan—opening of ports with consular representation and extraterritorial rights for Japanese subjects.

In the years following Japan gave considerable support to a party of Korean reformers who aimed at modernizing the administration of their country in imitation of Japan and at improving the conditions for trade and capital investment. A sharp conflict broke out between these reformers and the conservative Court party. The latter appealed to China for aid, and both China and Japan thus came to take sides in a Korean domestic struggle which was carried on in Seoul by devious methods of intrigue, conspiracy, and assassination. A *coup d'état* in 1882 put the pro-Chinese party in power and it retained control of the government until 1894 under the direction of the Chinese Resident in Seoul, the able and astute Yuan Shih-k'ai. An attempt of the

Reformists to seize power in 1884 was completely defeated after a momentary success.

The year 1884 also saw Russia's entry into the field of Korean politics. On the proposal of the German von Möllendorff, who had been lent by China to Korea as financial adviser, Korea concluded an agreement with Russia whereby Russian officers were to undertake the reorganization and training of the Korean army and Russia was to have the use of the ice-free harbour of Port Lazarev halfway down the east coast of Korea as a naval station. China, still engaged in her war with France, does not appear to have objected to this scheme, hoping, no doubt, that Russian influence could be played off against Japanese. But strong objection came from a quarter which China could not ignore—from London. The British Government, resolved to counter any Russian expansion south of Vladivostok, ordered the naval occupation of a group of small islands to the south of Korea known as Port Hamilton, and declined to evacuate them unless China gave a guarantee of the territorial integrity of Korea. England's action on this occasion followed the precedent of 1861, when the Russians had tried to present a *fait accompli* by the occupation of Tsushima. Russia likewise, being still without real strength in the Far East, followed the precedent of 1861 and disavowed any intention of taking a Korean port. Von Möllendorff was dismissed, the Russian officers did not arrive, and the British evacuated

Port Hamilton early in 1887. Russia's first move in Korea was thus a fiasco, but it foreshadowed the more successful attempt made in 1897 when Russia's power had been enormously increased by railway building, as well as by an alliance with China.

The withdrawal of Russia and England left China and Japan to continue their quarrel over the prostrate body of the Korean kingdom. In 1894 Korea was plunged into fresh confusion by the revolt of a religious sect known as the Tonghaks, and on an appeal from the Korean government China dispatched troops, informing Japan of her resolve to 'restore the peace of our tributary state'. Japan also landed troops in Korea and declared in reply to the Chinese communication that 'although the words "tributary state" appear in your note, the Imperial Government has never recognized Korea as a tributary state of China'. War followed with a Japanese naval attack on Chinese transports.

In the course of the war the Japanese destroyed or captured the greater part of the Chinese navy, drove the Chinese forces out of Korea, occupied southern Manchuria as far west as the Liao river, and invaded Shantung. Hopelessly defeated, China was compelled to sue for peace. But it was not only with China that Japan had to deal. The Western Powers with interests in China were concerned at the sudden upset of the *status quo* in the Far East, and it was clear that they could not be indifferent to the terms of peace between the victor and the vanquished. Russia showed her intention of obtaining respect for her wishes by dispatching twenty-one warships from European waters to the Pacific.

In spite of appeals from China, however, no intervention by any of the Western Powers took place during the peace negotiations, and the war was brought to an end by the Treaty of Shimonoseki signed on April 17, 1895. By this treaty Japan obtained not only a recognition by China of Korea's independence—the original matter in dispute—but also most-favoured-nation status for Japan in China (which automatically gave to Japan all rights and privileges possessed there by the Western Powers), certain additional rights not yet possessed by any foreign Power (which automatically became available for all nations endowed with most-favoured-nation status), a large indemnity and the cession in full sovereignty of Formosa, the Pescadores, and the Liaotung Peninsula of southern Manchuria with the harbour of Port Arthur at its extremity.

It was the last of these provisions which proved to be the bone of contention. Russia was determined not to be forestalled by Japan in Manchuria or Korea just at the moment when her capacity for Far Eastern expansion was about to mature. The Finance Minister Witte, the most influential person in the Russian Government at the time, declares in his *Memoirs* that he 'insisted on the necessity of thwarting the execution of the peace treaty between Japan and China'. This was to be done on the prin-

ciple that 'no Power be allowed to increase its territorial possessions at China's expense'. Russia persuaded France and Germany to join her in presenting
Japan with a joint demand for the retrocession to
China of the Liaotung Peninsula. The *démarche* of
the three Powers—the famous Triple Intervention—
was made in Tokyo on April 23, six days after the
signing of the Treaty of Shimonoseki. The Russian
memorandum declared that the Japanese possession
of Liaotung 'would mean a constant threat to the
capital of China, and at the same time would render
illusory the independence of Korea; and that it con-
stitutes accordingly a permanent obstacle in the way
of peace in the Far East'. The German Minister
with an unnecessary brutality of speech openly
threatened Japan with war. His two colleagues more
discreetly tendered advice 'as an expression of sin-
cere friendship', but whatever their effort to spare
Japanese pride, the reality behind their demands
consisted of their combined fleets available in the
Pacific, which were amply sufficient to sever communications between Japan and her army on the
mainland. Japan, moreover, in spite of her victories,
had been financially exhausted by the war, and was
in fact helpless against the forces of the Dreibund.
England had not joined in the intervention, but had
no intention of opposing it, and advised Japan to
yield. Japan made her submission and evacuated
Port Arthur, which the Power so zealous for China's
integrity was herself to occupy three years later.

The motives of France and Germany in supporting Russia have already been indicated in our preliminary consideration of the Dreibund as a grouping of the European Powers. France stood by Russia
in order to confirm her alliance. In Germany, on
the other hand, there were at first divided counsels,
such as are reflected in a memorandum from the
Chancellor to the Kaiser expounding the view that
'we must avoid letting ourselves be drawn prema-
turely into an action which serves primarily the
interests of others, but we must keep open to us
participation in such undertakings as may lead to
rearrangements in the balance of power of the
European Great Powers in Eastern Asia'. Germany's
policy was for a time non-committal, but soon inclined definitely to a pro-Russian course. 'It is a
question', wrote the Kaiser in a marginal comment
on a Foreign Office memorandum, 'of supporting
Russia in this matter for the sake of producing as
great a relief of pressure as possible upon our Eastern
border. . . . It is in our interest to direct Russia to
the East where her true mission lies.'

England had no incentive for departing from an
attitude of complete neutrality on this occasion.
She neither opposed nor supported Japan over the
Liaotung issue. She informed the German and
Russian Governments that 'Britain's interest in East
Asia was not sufficiently prejudiced by the Japanese
peace terms to justify an intervention, which appar-
ently could only be executed by force'. Japan had

been at great pains to secure the goodwill of England, first by deference to a British request not to conduct any warlike operations in the neighbourhood of Shanghai (an agreement involving a serious restriction for Japanese strategy in the war) and secondly, by obtaining from China in the Treaty of Shimonoseki certain concessions—such as the right to establish warehouses in the interior—which became available for British trade under the most-favoured-nation clause. Prevailing British opinion was, therefore, well disposed towards Japan, and expressed itself clearly in a *Times* editorial of April 8, which declared :

'It does not appear that there is any reason why this country, at any rate, should interfere to prevent the cession of this small corner of outlying Chinese territory to Japan. British interests, as far as we can see, are not in any way threatened by this stipulation, while by other parts of the agreement [the Shimonoseki Treaty] they may possibly be advanced. We have no title to meddle in these negotiations unless British interests are injured or imperilled.'

But if England was not alarmed at the prospect of a Japanese possession of Port Arthur, neither was she perturbed in the spring of 1895 by a fear of Russian expansion in the Far East. If she had anticipated the sequel to the Triple Intervention, she would certainly not have advised Japan to yield and failed to support her against the Dreibund. But Russia had been so long quiescent in the Far East and her

attempts to move forward in 1861 and 1884 had
been so easily checked that England was quite un-
prepared for the rapid evolution of Russian policy
after the Sino-Japanese war. It was not until the
autumn of 1895 that well-informed circles in
England became aware of the real significance of
the Triple Intervention and of Russia's plans in
Manchuria. It was then England's turn to be concerned about 'the small corner of outlying Chinese
territory'. Japan was not reckoned as a Great
Power, but Russia was—and a Power which neither
the British navy nor British finance could control.
The Far Eastern Question suddenly emerged, and
its gravity was at once appreciated. Russia, declared
The Times on October 25, commenting on a dispatch
from its Hong Kong correspondent,

'cannot possibly imagine that the other Great Powers
having interests in the Far East can view with indifference
an enterprise which would constitute a destruction of
the existing balance of power almost unparalleled in its
audacity. . . . It is obvious that with Russian fleets in the
harbour of Port Arthur and a railway connecting that
place with the Siberian trunk line, Manchuria would
practically become a Russian province, the Chinese
capital itself would be in Russia's grip, and every Power
in any degree interested in Chinese affairs would have
to effect a fundamental revision of the arrangements by
which its position and commercial interests are at present
secured.'

The Battle of the Concessions had begun.

VI

THE BATTLE OF THE CONCESSIONS

'IT is evident,' wrote the Russian Foreign Minister to the Russian Ambassador in Paris in a letter dated May 23, 1895, 'that after what we have done for China we wish to enable her to rid her territory as quickly as possible of the presence of the Japanese, and to this end to make it easy for her to obtain a loan. This motive, though very real, is not, however, the only one that prompts us. It is no less important for our future designs to have China in a state of dependence towards us and not to let England extend her influence there.'

The 'future designs' covered an ambitious programme of Far Eastern expansion. The idea was to gain control of Manchuria, and if possible of the Chinese empire as a whole, not as an invader and aggressor, but as China's ally and protector. China had been at war with Japan, was bitterly resentful at her humiliating defeat, and feared a renewal of Japanese encroachments. Japan was China's enemy; Russia would be her friend. Russia would fight to preserve China's integrity if Japan again advanced. But in order to act on behalf of China Russia would have to have the necessary strategic facilities, such as a railway across Manchuria prolonging the Trans-Siberian line, a right to use Chinese ports in time

of war, and, sooner or later, a naval base to be provided by China on the shore of the Yellow Sea.
With such a position Russia would be able to defend
China against Japan—and no one would be able to
defend China against Russia.

Russia began by joining with France in a 400-
million-franc loan to enable China to pay off the
first instalment of the indemnity due to Japan.
French banks put up most of the money, but the
loan was guaranteed by Russia. The next step was
to set up a Russo-Chinese Bank, in which French
financiers were the chief shareholders, but which was,
in the words of a Russian diplomat,[1] 'but a slightly
disguised branch of the Russian treasury'. The Bank
was empowered to undertake various financial transactions on behalf of the Chinese Government and
also to acquire 'concessions for the construction of
railways within the borders of China'. The creation
of the Bank was followed by the proposal to run the
Trans-Siberian railway through Manchuria in a
direct line from Chita to Vladivostok ; it was claimed
that the line would not only be of benefit to China's
trade, but would enable Russia rapidly to concentrate forces to aid China in another war with Japan.
To allay any suspicion of a threat to China's sovereignty it was laid down that the line should be
'constructed and exploited not by the Russian
Government, but by a commercial association concerning the constitution of which the two govern-

[1] Baron Rosen, *Forty Years of Diplomacy*, vol. i, p. 198.

ments would have to come to an agreement'.[1] In
spite of these arguments the Chinese Ministers are
said to have been 'smitten with a stupor by the proposal', and it might have been resisted had not Li
Hung-chang, who had been sent to Russia to attend
the coronation of the Tsar Nicholas II, been won
over by the promise of a formal Russo-Chinese alliance conditional on the acceptance of the railway
project. The Treaty of Alliance (which was secret)
was concluded in May 1896, and it provided for the
building of the railway across Manchuria to Vladivostok. There also appears to have been a grant for
an unnamed Chinese seaport terminus, implying a
branch line to the Yellow Sea. The latter part of
the scheme, however, was not meant to be put into
execution at once; it was necessary to build up Russian strength in central Manchuria before approaching the Yellow Sea, where strong opposition was to
be anticipated from rival Powers, and in any case
the Russian authorities were still in doubt as to what
port would be most convenient. The Russian navy
gained by the treaty the right to use all Chinese
ports in a war under the terms of the alliance, but
it still had no regular base south of Vladivostok.

The construction of the Trans-Manchurian line
was entrusted to the Russo-Chinese Bank, which
formed the Chinese Eastern Railway Company.
Shares were to be acquired only by Chinese or Russian subjects. An ingeniously framed contract gave

[1] A. Gerard, *Ma mission en Chine*, p. 137.

a nominal power of supervision to China but all effective control to the Russian Ministry of Finance and its nominees. The railway was to revert to the Chinese Government after eighty years, or it might be purchased by China after thirty-six. Meanwhile the Company was to have 'the absolute and exclusive right of administration of its lands', including its own police—to provide which Russian troops were presently introduced under the title of 'railway guards'.

Parallel with their penetration of Manchuria the Russians now also renewed their pressure on Korea. Russian prestige had been enormously enhanced by the Triple Intervention, and the anti-Japanese party in Seoul which had relied on China now turned towards Russia. Japan was powerless to prevent this development, and concluded an agreement with Russia, known as the Lobanov-Yamagata Treaty, whereby certain Japanese rights and privileges received recognition, but Russia gained the right to appoint a financial adviser to the Korean Government. A Russo-Korean Bank—a branch of the Russo-Chinese Bank—was founded in 1897.

France supported all these enterprises both financially and diplomatically. Her policy was directed first and foremost towards strengthening the bond of the Franco-Russian Alliance by proving her devotion to Russia's causes and her value as a friend. But she also had imperialist designs of her own in China. She did not regard her Far Eastern colonial account as closed. She had been forestalled by England in Burma in 1885 and checked again by England in Siam in 1893, but she saw possibilities of extending her colonial domain—with or without actual annexations of territory—by building a railway from Tongking to the upper Yangtse and thus diverting to a French port a great part of the trade of west and south-west China which had hitherto flowed down the Yangtse and Sikiang rivers to Shanghai and Hong Kong. The Chamber of Commerce of Lyons sent a mission in 1895 to explore the commercial and transport possibilities of the Chinese provinces adjacent to French Indo-China. The report of the mission expounded a policy which had been 'defined by the President of the Chamber of Commerce of Lyons, in one of those apt phrases of which he is a master, as the commercial "soldering" between our possessions and China'. The provinces to be 'soldered' to French Indo-China—or 'drained' thither (in another of the President's apt phrases)— were Kwangsi, Yunnan, Kweichow, and Szechwan, comprising over a quarter of the total area of China proper and nearly a fifth of its population. This grandiose scheme was never executed except for Yunnan, partly on account of the engineering difficulties which made railway construction in the mountainous south-west so much more expensive than on the broad plains of Manchuria or the north-eastern provinces of China, but still more because of the opposition of England which France was reluctant to provoke after 1898. During the years 1895–8, however, the plan was taken seriously, and France worked with Russia in diplomacy at Peking for a simultaneous penetration of China by railways running northward from Tongking and southward from Siberia.

In this promising partnership of Russia and France, Germany, whose support had been useful for intimidating Japan, was an unwanted third. Russia and France were anxious to exclude Germany from the benefits of their policies in China. Yet they could not go too far in flouting her or she might cross over to the camp of the arch-enemy, England. By giving support to England—or to Japan—Germany could certainly make difficulties for her Dreibund friends and thus acquire a nuisance value to induce them to give her a share in the Far Eastern spoil. On the other hand, if she were to join forces with England to the point of thwarting Russia in her Far Eastern ambitions—and she could not in the last resort combine with England on any other terms—she ran the risk of bringing about what she wished above all things to prevent—the return of Russia to an active, forward policy in Europe. Germany was thus faced with a dilemma which ultimately brought her to political disaster. If she had aimed simply at diverting Russia to the Far East, her policy must have been to give steady support to Russia on Chinese issues; alternatively, if she had merely been considering the promotion of her own interests in China, she could have pursued the policy most suitable to that end. But the endeavour to serve both purposes at once involved Germany in endless vacillations and contradictions and had a most damaging effect on her general diplomatic position.

Germany had been promised at the time of the Triple Intervention that German financiers would be admitted to participation in the loan to China for the payment of the indemnity to Japan. When the time came they were excluded, and Russia explained that France vetoed German participation. This was the first—and not the last—split in the Dreibund. Germany retaliated by giving diplomatic support to Japan on certain matters arising out of the execution of the Treaty of Shimonoseki and by joining England in negotiation for a loan to China to pay the second instalment of the indemnity. The loan was obtained by a syndicate of the Deutsch-Asiatische and the Hong Kong and Shanghai Banks. The conflict between Germany and the Franco-Russian group was accentuated when the former began to press a claim for a coaling station somewhere on the coast of China. At this time Germany had no *point d'appui* in the Far East, and was thus at a great disadvantage compared with other European Powers possessing territorial bases there. After the Triple Intervention she requested China to grant her a coaling station as a reward for her service. China refused on the ground that, if she were to grant it, other Powers would demand 'compensations'.

Germany was unwilling, however, to renounce her purpose, and began to come round to the view attributed to the Russian Minister in Peking, Count Cassini, that, 'if one wants anything in China, one must demand and take it without further ado'. It was decided 'to wait until the Chinese give us cause for reprisals', and then seize a place which would be not only convenient as a coaling station but also 'suitable as a starting-point for the establishment of a German Colonial territory'. This plan was not at all to the liking of France and Russia, who put pressure on the Chinese Government not to grant any such German demand. The French, fearing that Germany might gain a foothold on the island of Hainan or the Kwangtung coast between Canton and the French border, obtained from China a guarantee of non-alienation of that area, while the Russians maintained that the Russo-Chinese alliance precluded the grant of a Chinese port to a Power other than Russia. However, Germany had chosen Kiaochow Bay on the coast of Shantung as her goal and took action with her fleet. The 'cause for reprisals' having been provided by the murder of two German Catholic missionaries in Shantung, a German squadron sailed to Kiaochow and took possession in November 1897.

Russia at once protested, claiming a prior right of anchorage at Kiaochow. Confronted by strong opposition from Russia, Germany turned to England. The German Ambassador in London hinted that

Germany might have to purchase Russian consent to her occupation by entering an anti-British coalition, unless England would support Germany. England took up an attitude of benevolent neutrality, and Germany approached Russia with proposals for German support of compensation for Russia at China's expense. The Russians after unsuccessfully trying to get concessions from China in return for a promise of assistance against Germany, accepted the German offer, and sent a squadron to anchor in the harbour of Port Arthur. The Russian Foreign Minister, Count Muraviev, held that 'the occupation of Kiaochow by the Germans offered a favourable occasion for us to seize one of the Chinese ports, notably Port Arthur or the adjacent Talienwan', and later on, after the acquisition of these places, he remarked to the German Ambassador that Russia could only be grateful to Germany, as she 'could hardly have found an opportunity' for her action but for the German seizure of Kiaochow.

The united front of the Dreibund was thus restored, but it was now directed against China and no longer on her behalf. At Peking the German and Russian representatives demanded long leases of Kiaochow and Port Arthur (with Talienwan) respectively. The Germans were already in occupation of Kiaochow, and in making a formal cession China was only resigning herself to an accomplished fact. The Russians on the other hand had not actually occupied Port Arthur, as they desired to preserve the form of the Russo-Chinese alliance by making the cession appear as a voluntary grant; they claimed Port Arthur as a means of carrying out their obligation to defend China. China objected and had to be persuaded by a naval demonstration plus a bribe of half a million roubles to Li Hung-chang. The grant of Kiaochow was made on March 6, 1898, and that of Port Arthur on March 27. Both Germany and Russia were pleased with their bargain, and the Kaiser declared in a message to the Tsar that 'Russia and Germany at the entrance of the Yellow Sea may be taken as represented by St. George and St. Michael shielding the Holy Cross in the Far East and guarding the gates to the continent of Asia'.

The taking of Kiaochow and Port Arthur on lease marked a new departure in the methods of European imperialism in the Far East. Hitherto territory had been annexed in full sovereignty by European Powers, as in the cases of Hong Kong, the Primorsk and Annam. But the effective autonomy developed by the foreign settlements in China, and especially by the International Settlement at Shanghai, had suggested that formal sovereignty was not necessary for the exercise of sovereign rights in China, and leasehold tenure provided a convenient device whereby foreign Powers might acquire the substance of colonial authority without a complete transfer of title. No foreign Power has in fact taken territory from China in full sovereignty since 1895.

A system of semi-sovereign rights of an essentially colonial character has been elaborated on Chinese soil, and has produced that extraordinary overlapping of state authorities which was destined to confront the world with a baffling political dilemma after the Covenant of the League of Nations had guaranteed 'the territorial integrity and existing political independence of all members of the League' and Chinese nationalism had started its campaign for 'recovery of rights'. Actually, the leased territories in China were the colonies of the Powers that held them and, together with 'railway zones' attached to them, formed enclaves of foreign dominion destructive of China's sovereignty. The occupying Powers had full rights of administration, police, and defence, and their ports became fortified military and naval bases, from which they could either coerce China or make war on each other. The existence of these bases rendered Chinese territory outside the leased areas liable to invasion, even in quarrels to which China was not a party, for wartime strategy could not be expected to take account of the narrow leasehold boundaries. The Kiaochow lease was for ninety-nine years, that of Port Arthur for twenty-five, to be 'prolonged subsequently by mutual consent' of Russia and China. Both Russia and Germany, however, regarded the acquisitions as permanent and China's reversionary rights as merely nominal. In connexion with the Kiaochow leasehold the Germans obtained the right to

P

construct two railway lines in Shantung, mining properties and a preferential right to all kinds of investment concessions in the province—thus making it their 'sphere'—while the Russians obtained the right to build a railway linking Port Arthur with their main transcontinental line at Harbin and guarantees that no other Power should be granted railway concessions or an open port in the vicinity.

These were the gains of Germany and Russia. France followed next with demands backed by a threat of force and supported diplomatically by Russia. By an exchange of notes with China France obtained, on April 10, the promise of a lease of a bay on the south coast of China, a concession for a railway from Tongking to Yunnan city, a guarantee of non-alienation for Kwangtung, Kwangsi, and Yunnan provinces, and the post of Director of Chinese Posts for a French national. France chose for her leasehold the bay of Kwangchow-wan on the Kwangtung coast about midway between the French Indo-China border and Hong Kong.

This was not, however, the end of China's troubles. The unhappy Court of Peking had also to reckon with England. England, having her own territorial base in Hong Kong and a two-thirds share of the total foreign trade of China, was the protagonist of the open door and free commercial competition in China. On January 17, 1898, after it had become known that Russia was pressing for a lease of Port Arthur, the Chancellor of the Exchequer, Sir M.

Hicks-Beach, declared in a speech that 'the Government was absolutely determined, at whatever cost, even—and he wished to speak plainly—if necessary, at the cost of war, that the door should not be shut against us'. In a parliamentary debate on March 1 the Government announced itself 'opposed to the alienation of any portion of Chinese territory or to the sacrifice of any part of Chinese independence'. A month later, however—on April 2—England obtained from China by threat of naval action the lease of Weihaiwei on the Shantung coast north of Kiaochow. The leases of Kiaochow and Port Arthur had been granted in the meantime, and after the cession of Port Arthur, against which she had protested in vain, England exchanged the policy of maintaining China's integrity for one of demands for compensation. It was easier to threaten war against China than against France and Russia, and the British Government decided to join in the China-devouring scramble which it was not in a position to prevent.

Weihaiwei was chosen as the place most suitable for a British *point d'appui* against Russian power in the region of the Yellow Sea. It had been captured by Japan in the war of 1894 and was still occupied by the Japanese as security against the fulfilment of the peace terms, but was due shortly to be evacuated. It was also in Shantung, which Germany now claimed as her sphere of influence. It was necessary, therefore, for England to conciliate both Japan and Germany, if the taking of Weihaiwei was not to involve serious complications. In the middle of March inquiry was made in Tokyo whether a British lease of Weihaiwei would be agreeable to Japan, and Japan replied cautiously that she had 'no objection to its possession by a Power disposed to assist in maintaining the independence of China'. Japan only asked for the 'concurrence and support of England' for any similar measure she might take in the future 'to strengthen her defences or to promote her interests'. The squaring of Germany was more difficult. To placate Germany and detach her from Russia, England had to recognize the German enclosure of Shantung—a radical modification of her traditional policy, for she had not hitherto admitted any exceptions to the most-favoured-nation principle or any restriction on the competitive enterprise of British subjects in China. At this cost England was able to obtain Weihaiwei without meeting united opposition from the Dreibund. At the same time, she demanded and obtained from China in compensation for the cession of Kwangchow-wan to France a lease of territory adjacent to Hong Kong which the Admiralty judged to be necessary for the defence of the colony.

England thus restored, as far as coastal bases were concerned, the balance of power which had been upset by the German, Russian, and French gains. But the climax of the Battle of the Concessions was yet to come. The summer of 1898 saw the political storm-centre shift from the question of leased territories to that of spheres of influence. A 'sphere of influence'was the term used for a region of the Chinese empire within which a particular foreign Power was granted a preferential or exclusive right to capital investment enterprises, especially concessions for railway construction.   England, having recognized Germany's claim to an exclusive sphere in Shantung, could no longer oppose sphere-making on principle, and her interests required that she should have a sphere of her own, since it was no longer possible to maintain the open door for the whole of China. As Mr. Balfour declared with regard to the Russian veto on British railway enterprise in Manchuria, 'Her Majesty's Government cannot possibly acquiesce in an arrangement which leaves all China open to the railway enterprises of Russia, while excluding England from her share in the railway enterprises of Manchuria'.

To ease the shock to the British public of so sudden a transition from open-door to monopoly economics, Mr. Balfour invented a hair-splitting distinction between a 'sphere of influence' and a 'sphere of interest', the latter being deemed to possess a virtue which was lacking in the former.   But influence or interest, England was in fact determined that if she were driven to enclose, she would do it in the grand manner. She claimed for her sphere nothing less than the whole basin of the Yangtse with well over half the total population of the Chinese empire. From this area England now endeavoured to exclude non-British, and especially French or Russian, railway enterprise. But the Chinese Government had already promised the concession for the all-important line from Peking to Hankow on the middle Yangtse to a Belgian syndicate. On inquiry from the British Government, China gave an assurance that the Russo-Chinese Bank was in no way concerned in the enterprise, but in August it became known that the terms of the contract actually gave this arm of the Russian state an important interest in it. A protest was thereupon made to Peking, but, under strong pressure from France and Russia, China ratified the contract on August 12.

England retaliated by demanding concessions for *five* projected railways, including one which was calculated to compete closely with the Peking-Hankow line. The British minister in Peking was instructed, 'after consultation with the Admiral', to present these demands in the form of an ultimatum, and informed that 'unless they [the Chinese] agree at once, we shall regard their breach of faith concerning the Peking-Hankow Railway as an act of deliberate hostility against this country and shall act accordingly'. The Minister announced that he had received from London 'telegraphic instructions of the gravest character', and the Chinese Government, aware of the fleet movements which had been ordered, immediately capitulated.

It was clear at this point that the process of extortion and counter-extortion at the expense of China had reached the limit that was compatible with peace between the rival European Powers. China was powerless to resist, but each fresh surrender increased the danger of a major conflict between the concession-seekers. There was the risk that the procedure of ultimatum, which in the last few months had become normal in Far Eastern affairs, would be used once too often, and that a great European war would be precipitated by one of the recurring clashes between England and Russia. The situation was full of peril for England. At the end of an epoch of 'splendid isolation' she was without an ally, menaced by a powerful European coalition, and embarrassed by the conflict with the Boer republics in South Africa. In the actual course of events, however, the tension in China was greatly relaxed in the autumn of 1898, and the international situation turned in favour of England. This was not immediately apparent because September saw the commencement of the Fashoda crisis in Anglo-French relations, and it seemed that the threatened war was about to break out, not indeed on a Far Eastern, but on an African, issue. 'C'était bien de guerre qu'il s'agissait', writes de Freycinet,[1] and it was certainly a period of severe strain. But war did not come, and the results of the bitter quarrel were just the opposite of what might have been expected. Instead of accentuating the antagonism of the Franco-Russian group versus England, the Fashoda episode diminished it. The clash in the Sudan diverted the attention of

[1] *La Question d'Égypte*, p. 413.

France from China to Africa and loosened her tie
with Russia, for whereas both Russia and France
had interests in China, Russia had none in Central
Africa, and showed a lukewarmness in supporting
France in this crisis which left Frenchmen with a
vivid sense of the limitations of the alliance. Further,
France came up against the brutal fact of British
naval supremacy which she had tended to underestimate. It is hard for a continental nation, inevitably preoccupied with land frontiers and military
establishments, to appreciate in normal times the
possible modes of operation of sea-power. It is only
when directly confronted with superior naval strength
in relation to overseas colonies that such a nation
fully apprehends the reality called 'command of the
sea'. France had this experience in 1898–9, and the
humiliation she underwent led her ultimately to
the *Entente cordiale*. France now understood that, in
the event of a war of the Franco-Russian alliance
against England, France with her vulnerable sea
communications would get all the knocks, while the
gains, if any, would go to all-continental Russia.
Henceforth France sought to avoid conflict with England, and, while continuing to adhere to the Russian
alliance, to use her diplomacy for the mitigation of
Anglo-Russian antagonism.

The other main factor favourable to England in
the autumn of 1898 was her new friendship with the
United States, which dated from August 13, when a
British admiral interposed his flagship between the

German and American squadrons in Manila Bay, thus dissuading the former from its threatened intervention in the Spanish-American war. The American occupation of the Philippines meant that the United States had for the first time a territorial extension in the Far East, implying both a new stake of interest and an increase of regional power. From 1898 onwards the U.S.A. was a major factor in the Far Eastern situation, whereas hitherto she had played but a small part except for her initiative in opening Japan. It was fortunate for England that this entry of America into Far Eastern affairs coincided with a marked improvement of Anglo-American relations, which had recently been subjected to a severe strain by mutual recriminations over the Guiana-Venezuela boundary dispute. The danger to America during the war of 1898 was never from Spain, against whom she required no aid, but from Germany, who saw an opportunity of increasing her colonial empire by the seizure of the Philippines, where a successful native revolt against Spain was already in progress. A German squadron under Diedrichs proceeded to Manila, ignoring the American blockade regulations, and assumed a menacing attitude towards the less powerful American fleet operating against the city. At the critical moment the manœuvre of the British admiral, who was also present with a squadron, rendered it impossible for the German ships to open fire on the Americans without also firing on the British. This support was much appreciated by the American Government, which at one time believed war with Germany to be imminent, and when it was decided to retain the Philippines under American sovereignty, the value of British friendship for the protection of the new colony was clearly perceived in Washington. For British policy in the Far East American friendship provided a no less welcome reinforcement, and co-operation between the two Powers was made easy by the convergence of their interests in China *vis-à-vis* the Dreibund nations and their enclosure policies. Lacking any common land frontier with China or coastal base in China or apparatus of government suitable for sustained imperialist activity, the U.S.A. could not hope to come off well in the scramble for the partition of China into monopolist spheres. Her commercial interest demanded the 'open door'. England likewise desired the restoration of the 'open door', but having laid claim to a sphere herself, was no longer in a good moral position for denouncing the enclosure system, and in 1899 America became the protagonist of what had been England's policy.

VII

THE ANGLO-JAPANESE ALLIANCE

AFTER the political storm which had raged through the spring and summer of 1898 the situation in the Far East was stabilized for a while on a new basis. No really satisfactory settlement was reached, but there was a temporary relaxation of the conflict, and when the struggle was renewed its form had changed considerably. The settlement, such as it was, consisted of two parts, the first concerned with spheres of capital investment and the second with conditions of trade. To the former category belong the Anglo-German and Anglo-Russian sphere agreements concluded between August of '98 and May of '99, and to the latter the acceptance, by all the 'China Powers' except Russia, of the 'open door doctrine', as enunciated by Secretary Hay of the United States in a circular appeal to the interested governments in September 1899.

The principle of the open door, in the early days of foreign economic penetration of China, had meant simply that the conditions of residence and charges, such as customs duties and harbour dues, must be equal for all nations trading with China, and that China was bound not to discriminate or give preferential treatment. With equal conditions established, buying and selling could be carried on in a free market between individual traders and firms.

There was little difficulty in the application of the principle as long as only commercial transactions were in question; it was when foreigners in China began to undertake enterprises involving large investments of capital and contracts with the Chinese Government that complications arose. In pure economic theory there was no reason why the open door principle should be less applicable to these enterprises than to ordinary commercial exchange, no reason why contractors should not compete with their tenders for railway or mining concessions just as the traders competed in buying tea or selling cloth. In practice, however, the concessions could not be kept apart from international politics; the negotiations were carried on through, or with the aid of, government representatives, and political considerations intruded at every turn. Concessions were obtained as rewards for diplomatic aid or were extorted by pressure and menaces. It was not only the profits of these enterprises which were at stake. Railway lines linked with territorial bases were of great strategic significance in view of China's weakness and the widely held expectation of her collapse as an organized state. It was impossible to ignore the political problems involved in the granting of such concessions or to pretend that it was decided solely in accordance with an economic law of supply and demand. The theory of the open door was forced to yield to the facts of enclosure and politically promoted investment monopolies. A distinction thus

came to be drawn in England between purely commercial transactions, to which the principle of the
open door was still held to apply, and investment
concessions, for which a principle of geographical
partition might be recognized. The new doctrine
was stated by the Duke of Devonshire in a speech
in the autumn of 1898.

'As to the ordinary operations of trade, we hold that we
are entitled to the utmost of our power to maintain our
rights to the principle of equal opportunities for all. But
as to enterprises, or the development by capital proceed-
ing from other countries, Lord Salisbury has pointed out
that absolute equality is not possible in such cases because
it is not possible that different persons can have the same
concession in the same place.'

As thus expressed the argument was fallacious,
and its authors were doubtless well aware that it
was. The purpose of the propaganda which made
use of it was to conceal the real character of the
'sphere of interest' in the Yangtse valley which England was now striving to enclose. The question was
not whether Russian and English contractors could
simultaneously hold a concession for building a railway from X to Y, but whether they should have an
equal right to tender for it, and it was this that the
system of spheres denied, for its principle was to give
to each nation an exclusive or preferential right in
a particular part of China. There was, nevertheless,
a very real distinction between trade in goods and
investment concessions, and in the circumstances it

was a good practical policy for the British Government to seek different types of regulation for the two categories of economic activity.

The system of railway concession spheres was established by Anglo-German and Anglo-Russian agreements. The British Government had in April given a qualified endorsement to the German claim to a sphere in Shantung in order to avert an alignment of Germany with Russia in opposition to the British occupation of Weihaiwei. In September an agreement between British and German banking groups with the approval of their respective governments confirmed and extended the German claims and gave recognition to British pretensions with regard to the Yangtse valley. An agreement with Russia was harder to obtain, but at last, by an exchange of notes on April 28, 1899, England undertook not to seek railway concessions north of the Great Wall and Russia not to seek them in the basin of the Yangtse.

While thus accepting the sphere system for railway construction, England strove to reassert the open door for trade. This required that no differential rates be applied as regards customs tariffs, harbour dues, and railway freight charges in the leased territories and spheres of interest of the several Powers. Such conditions of commerce were necessary for England if her existing trade was not to be throttled in the regions served by French, Russian, or German ports and railways. For American commerce they

were even more essential, as the U.S.A. had neither
a coastal territory nor a recognized sphere of interest.
It was the American Government, therefore, which
took the initiative in a great effort to obtain from
the Powers concerned a declaration of resolve to adhere to the open-door policy as regards trade. The
move was successful in obtaining satisfactory answers
from all the Powers addressed except one. England,
France, Germany, Italy, and Japan agreed to the
American proposal. Russia, however, gave a non-
committal and evasive reply. The other Powers,
who had all made their acceptances conditional on
general agreement, chose to regard the Russian
answer as affirmative, but the interview between
Count Muraviev and the American Ambassador left
no doubt as to the real intentions of the Russian
Government. The Russian Foreign Minister 'flew
into a passion and insisted upon it that Russia would
never bind herself in that way'.

The expansionist clique in St. Petersburg had certainly no intention of renouncing in any way the
fruits of the conquest to which it looked forward;
the territories to be controlled by Russia were to
be brought within her ultra-protectionist economic
system. The Russian Government—in so far as it
was a Government at all, for the various depart-
ments of state constantly pursued divergent policies—
aimed at the domination of China through military
power, and at the extraction by monopoly of profits
which the economic backwardness of Russia would

not enable her to win under free-trade conditions. The menace to British trade was well understood in London, and it was for this reason that the Russian acquisition of Port Arthur with its immense strategic possibilities caused such consternation. In the words of Joseph Chamberlain :

'It is not a question of a single province, it is a question of the whole fate of the Chinese Empire, and our interests in China are so great, our proportion of the trade is so enormous, and the potentialities of that trade so gigantic that I feel that no more vital question has ever been presented for the decision of a Government and the decision of a nation.'

A Russian sphere in Manchuria, even if commercially monopolist, was not by itself a serious matter for England. Manchuria was a relatively unimportant market, its population being still scanty except in a limited area of the south, and much of the trade naturally going to Russia for reasons of geography. What was to be feared, however, was an effective Russian occupation of Manchuria which would enable them to dominate the Chinese capital. Russian control of Manchuria would mean control of Peking, and Russian control of Peking, which sea-power alone could not prevent, would mean a virtual Russian protectorate over the decadent Manchu-Chinese empire. Other nations would have either to submit to a policy of Peking dictated from St. Petersburg or attempt to detach parts of China as colonies for themselves by the use of military force.

Everything turned, therefore, on the position in Manchuria. The Russians had now a base at Port Arthur which they were busy turning into a fortress, and soldiers as guards along their railways, but there was as yet no large concentration of Russian troops, no general occupation of the country and no through traffic on the railways, sections of which had still to be completed. The consolidation of Russian power required the completion of the railways and a full military occupation of Manchuria. The latter could not be accomplished secretly and would involve a deliberate challenge to all nations unwilling to see a Russian supremacy over China. Had the Russians not been presented by the course of events with a perfect excuse for occupying Manchuria, they might long have delayed to cross the Rubicon and many doubts and vacillations at St. Petersburg would doubtless have weakened Russian policy. But the Boxer outbreak of 1900 almost compelled Russian imperialism to accomplish its desire.

To the astonishment of European Foreign Offices China suddenly attempted to intervene in her own destiny. She had since 1894 been cast for a merely passive rôle; she was expected to submit to demands and to fulfil the obligations imposed by treaties. But the humiliation of the defeat by Japan and the ensuing exactions of the Western Powers had produced a ferment of opinion in China, and a strong patriotic feeling had been aroused, which in one section of the ruling class led to a movement

R

for reform on the lines so successfully followed by Japan, and in another fostered the idea of getting rid of all foreigners in China by a sort of St. Bartholomew's massacre and returning to the old ways of seclusion and self-sufficiency.

In 1898 the party of reform led by K'ang Yu-wei gained the ear of the Emperor Kwang Hsü, and a series of administrative and educational innovations were introduced by imperial decree. But too many prejudices and vested interests were disturbed; a reactionary coup destroyed or scattered the reforming statesmen, the Emperor was made a prisoner in his own palace, and the Empress-Dowager Tze Hsi, who had ruled during his minority, resumed the reins of power. The conservatives now had their opportunity to try *their* solution for China's woes. They allied themselves with the secret society of the Patriotic Harmony Fists—nicknamed 'Boxers'. This organization was centred in Shantung, where there was a strong popular resistance to the Germans. The anti-foreign movement, encouraged by Court circles, soon got out of control, leading to murders of foreign missionaries and persecution of converts, and finally to an attack on the foreign Legations in Peking and settlements at Tientsin. Troops and marines of various foreign Powers were landed and fought their way through to Tientsin, and on to Peking, meeting with resistance not only from Boxer bands but also from Chinese regular troops who had joined them. Finally the whole of the metropolitan province of Chihli (now Hopei) was occupied by a composite international force under the supreme command of a German, Count von Waldersee. Meanwhile Manchuria, where the Boxers had also risen and attacked foreigners, was occupied by a purely Russian army sent in from Siberia. In taking action there the Russians were merely doing their share for the common cause of all who were threatened by the indiscriminate anti-foreignism of the Boxers, and no objection could be taken to their military measures, but as soon as the trouble had subsided, it became apparent that they had come into Manchuria to stay. The other European Powers, who could only maintain their expeditionary forces in Peking by long sea communications, were anxious to withdraw them as soon as a settlement could be reached and order restored. The Russians discovered, however, that Manchuria was so inherently disorderly that evacuation might have to be indefinitely postponed.

As Russia consolidated her military position in the Far East, England came to feel more and more the need for an ally. It was the conflict with Russia in the Far East which first impelled England to reconsider her traditional policy of 'splendid isolation'. English public opinion was much more impressed by the experience of the Boer War, when the general hostility of the Continental press was a fact which could not be ignored, but the disadvantages and dangers of isolation were appreciated in an influential, though limited, circle from the time of the

Russian occupation of Port Arthur. Joseph Chamberlain in his speech of May 13, 1898, already quoted, clearly indicated the new orientation of policy when he said :

'History shows us that unless we are allied to some great military Power, as we were in the Crimean War, when we had France and Turkey as our allies, we cannot seriously injure Russia, although it may also be true that she cannot seriously injure us. . . . If the policy of isolation, which has hitherto been the policy of this country, is to be maintained in the future, then the fate of the Chinese empire may be, probably will be, hereafter decided without reference to our wishes and in defiance of our interests. If, on the other hand, we are determined to enforce the policy of the open door, . . . we must not reject the idea of an alliance with those Powers whose interests most nearly approximate to our own.'

Of the Powers with important interests in China, France and the United States could be dismissed from consideration, the former because she was an ally of Russia, and the latter because, though ready to give diplomatic support to England on the open door issue, she was isolationist on principle and was in any case, like England, almost exclusively a naval, and not a military, Power. There remained Germany and Japan. An alliance with the latter was not at first seriously considered. Japan was regarded as the most efficient of Asiatic states, but as a second-class Power nevertheless, and likely to prove more of a liability than an asset in a political combination. It was to Germany, therefore, that English statesmen instinctively turned, and between the spring of 1898 and the autumn of 1901 England repeatedly sought an understanding with Germany which would enable the two nations to make common cause against Russia in the Far East.

England was prepared to offer Germany a settlement of various colonial differences to her advantage and the advancement of her interests in China. As long as Germany had no large navy to support her overseas expansion she was dependent on England for such favours. But the price to be paid was Germany's entry into an anti-Russian combine, and this was contrary to Germany's policy of taking the sting out of the Franco-Russian alliance by encouraging Russian ambitions in the Far East. 'I don't want to bar the advance of the Russians', wrote the Kaiser in a marginal note on the report of Count Hatzfeldt's conversations with Chamberlain. 'The more the Russians get involved in Asia, the quieter they are in Europe.' And to the Tsar the Kaiser wrote: 'The English are trying hard, as far as I can make out, to find a continental army to fight for their interests. But I fancy they won't easily find one, at least not *mine*!'

In a memorandum written on March 2, 1899, Count von Bülow declared: 'We seek, in so far as it does not compromise our dignity, and without prejudice to our status, to avoid conflicts between third Powers. This applies especially to the great Anglo-Russian conflict of interests.'

Nevertheless, in 1900 Germany and England did for a short time come together in opposition to Russia. As Russia contributed the largest number of troops to the international expedition against the Boxers, she claimed the right of supreme command, but the Kaiser was extremely anxious that the post should be held by a German and England supported the German pretension. This led to friction between Germany and Russia, and Germany drew nearer to England. In an exchange of notes on October 16, 1900, England obtained an agreement for co-operation in maintaining the integrity of China and the open door to trade 'wherever both Powers can exert influence'. But when early in the following year England proposed a joint protest to Russia regarding Russian actions in Manchuria, Germany contended that the agreement did not apply to Manchuria, but only to China proper. 'Nothing can be more indifferent to us,' declared the German Chancellor in the Reichstag on March 15, 1901, 'than what happens in Manchuria. There are no real German interests there. We only watch over German interests in China, and we leave it to England to look after her own.'

After this the British Government despaired of getting adequate support from Germany. Negotiations for an alliance continued, but the thoughts of English statesmen were turning towards the idea of an alternative pact. Baron von Eckardstein, then German Chargé d'Affaires in London, who acted as go-between in the Anglo-German negotiations, thought that a triple alliance of England, Germany, and Japan might be arranged, and that the Berlin Foreign Office could be more easily won for such a combination than for a simple Anglo-German alliance which would involve greater commitments for Germany. He therefore suggested to the Japanese Ambassador in London, Baron Hayashi, that Japan should approach England with a tentative proposal for such an alliance. Hayashi consulted his Government and was instructed on April 16 to explore the possibilities of an agreement without unduly committing himself, as the policy of Tokyo was still in doubt.

There was a sharp division of opinion in Japan on the main question of foreign policy. An influential group strongly advocated the quest of a European ally to counter the power of Russia, and such an ally could only be England. Another group, however, led by Japan's most eminent statesman, Marquis Ito, held that Japan was not strong enough to challenge Russia, that an alliance with England would involve more risk than security, and that Japan's proper course was to come to terms with Russia on the principle of Russian supremacy in Manchuria and Japanese supremacy in Korea. Repeated efforts had been made to conclude an agreement with Russia on this basis, but had met with no success. Thus in 1898 Japan had submitted a proposal in which the Government 'declared its

willingness to consider Manchuria with its littoral
as being entirely outside the sphere of Japanese
interests, provided the Russian Government was
prepared to make the same declaration with regard
to Korea'. The Russian Government, however,
while expressing its 'great satisfaction' at the Japanese
attitude on Manchuria, declined to give any such
assurance with regard to Korea. The truth was that
the Russians despised Japan as a military Power,
and did not see any need for making concessions in
order to conciliate her.

In spite of rebuffs Marquis Ito clung to the idea
of securing Japanese supremacy in Korea by means
of understanding with Russia. As Prime Minister
in April 1901, he gave his consent to the tentative
negotiations in London, but he did not abandon
hope of getting results from the alternative policy.
On May 10 his Cabinet fell and in June Viscount
Katsura, who was more favourable to an alliance
with England, took office. Ito, being now without
any official position, but still the best known abroad
of Japanese statesmen, proposed that he should himself visit St. Petersburg on his way back from America
(where he was due shortly to receive an honorary
degree from Yale University) and find out what
offer Russia could be induced to make on the Korean
question. Katsura agreed to this plan, apparently
in order that Ito should not in future be able to say
that an opportunity of coming to terms with Russia
had been neglected. Ito left Tokyo in the middle of

September and after his visit to New Haven, Conn., proceeded to St. Petersburg by way of Paris. Meanwhile the alliance negotiations in London had progressed to the stage of a draft treaty. Ito's avoidance of London on his world tour was not, however, unknown to the British Foreign Secretary, who was not convinced by Hayashi's explanation that 'the Marquis could not come to London in November, because in that month the London climate was at its worst, and fogs were general and would prejudice Marquis Ito's health'. Lord Lansdowne inquired 'why, if he was travelling for his health, did he go to St. Petersburg in the winter'. The Japanese Ambassador had to obtain from Tokyo an explicit denial that Ito was on any official mission before the negotiations could proceed. Katsura was by now fully committed to the policy of the English alliance. Ito failed to obtain from Russia an offer sufficiently alluring to justify his opposition to the English alliance, and finally gave his support to it. On January 30, 1902, the Anglo-Japanese Treaty of Alliance was signed.

The Treaty declared that the signatories were actuated 'solely by a desire to maintain the *status quo* and general peace in the Extreme East', to uphold 'the independence and territorial integrity of the Empire of China and the Empire of Korea', and 'to secure equal opportunities in those countries for the commerce and industry of all nations'. England was said to have special interests in China, and Japan

s

both in China and 'in a peculiar degree, politically as well as commercially and industrially' in Korea. If either signatory acting in defence of the interests thus recognized were to be involved in a war with one other Power, the ally was to remain neutral, but if with two or more Powers, the ally was to join in the war. The effect of these provisions was to ensure Japan by the protection of British sea-power against a hostile intervention of France or Germany or both in case of a Russo-Japanese war. The Triple Intervention could not now be repeated without war against the combined forces of England and Japan. The advantage to England lay in the check imposed on Russia's southward expansion in the Far East by the definite pro-British alignment of Japan. As to the value of Japan's aid from a naval and military point of view, there was already a considerable divergence of English from Continental European opinion. Japan's capacity for making war was much more highly rated in England than in Russia, France, or Germany, and the martial test of 1904 gave the verdict in favour of the English estimate.

It had originally been intended to leave the pact open for the adherence of Germany. But Germany was never invited to join. By the middle of 1901 it was clear that friction between England and Germany was increasing instead of diminishing. Lord Lansdowne insisted that the Anglo-Japanese negotiations should be carried to completion before any new approach was made to Germany. They were brought to a successful issue, but meanwhile, on January 8, 1902, Count von Bülow as German Chancellor had delivered his famous 'biting on granite' speech in the Reichstag, and the Anglo-German *rapprochement* was definitely at an end. The grouping England-Japan-Germany was destined to remain a might-have-been, and instead of it the war of 1914 found the Anglo-Japanese and Franco-Russian alliances linked together in an anti-German coalition.

VIII

THE REPULSE OF RUSSIA

CONFRONTED with the Anglo-Japanese alliance and aware of the increasing reluctance of France to risk a conflict with England, the Russian Government felt a need for caution and decided to make a gesture of conciliation. On April 8, 1902, it concluded a convention with China whereby it agreed to withdraw its troops from Manchuria (outside the Port Arthur leased territory) in three stages, at intervals of six months. The first stage, the evacuation of the south-western part of Mukden province up to the Liao river, was faithfully carried out by October 1902. In April 1903, however, when the troops should have been withdrawn from the rest of Mukden and Kirin provinces, they were not only remaining there but were being heavily reinforced. Russia had gained a year for making war preparations, and was no longer going to be tied to her treaty obligation. As a leading Russian newspaper put it, 'one may make political mistakes, but that is no reason why one should persist in them'.

All through the year 1903 the Russians kept on sending ships, men, and guns to reinforce their establishment in the Far East. 'We have force on our side', declared the St. Petersburg *Novosti*, 'and resources sufficient to solve the most difficult problems'. Meanwhile, the Japanese were hurrying to completion a programme of naval building and purchase which was to provide them for the first time with a really powerful fleet. In this atmosphere of increasing tension diplomatic negotiations were carried on between Japan and Russia, beginning with a submission of proposals by Japan in August. No agreement was reached, and the Russian Government made long delays in replying to Japanese communications. Then at the beginning of February, 1903, Tokyo received news that a fresh Russian squadron was *en route* to the Far East from the Mediterranean, and a seven-hour council meeting of Cabinet Ministers and Elder Statesmen in the presence of the Emperor Meiji decided on war. On February 6 Japan broke off diplomatic relations, and on the night of February 8 Japanese torpedo boats attacked the Russian fleet in the outer roadstead of Port Arthur, disabling two battleships and a cruiser. Formal declarations of war were exchanged on February 10.

In spite of her long-continued preparations for war Russia was unready for it when it came. The Russian War Office had no conception of the gravity of the situation, and had taken no trouble to find out the extent of Japan's military resources. Russia, using her war preparations as a menace to back her diplomacy and confident up to the last that the Japanese would not dare to attack, now suddenly discovered that her forces were outnumbered in the

actual theatre of operations, and that the Japanese
war machine was working with speed and efficiency.
In the nine years since the Triple Intervention Japan
had been quietly putting into effect the programme
expounded by Count Hayashi (who afterwards negotiated the Anglo-Japanese alliance).

'We must continue', he wrote in 1895, 'to study according
to Western methods, for the application of science is the
most important item of warlike preparations that civilized
nations regard. If new ships of war are considered
necessary, we must build them at any cost. If the
organization of our army is found to be wrong, it must
at once be renovated. If advisable, our whole military
system must be entirely changed. We must build docks
to be able to repair our ships. We must establish a steel
factory to supply guns and ammunition. Our railways
must be extended so that we can mobilize our troops
rapidly. Our oversea shipping must be developed so
that we can provide transports to carry our armies
abroad. This is the programme that we have to keep
always in view. We have suffered hard things, and we
must suffer yet harder things before we arrive at our
destiny.'

The years between 1895 and 1904 were indeed
years of steady preparation and organization of the
Japanese nation for war. The modern Japanese
state and economic system acquired their characteristic features during this period. The subordination
of all political and economic life to the achievement
of war-power—a subordination rendered possible by
a general sense of impending crisis and national peril

—meant a concentration of military-bureaucratic control and a recession of the liberal-democratic tendencies which had been gaining ground before 1894. The rule that the War and Navy ministries in the Cabinet could be held only by generals and admirals on the active list was introduced on the demand of Marshal Yamagata to secure priority in the budget for the needs of the fighting services. War-power industries were built up through a system of state intervention and quasi-monopolist concessions, requirements being too urgent to leave economic development to the unregulated processes of private capital accumulation and investment. All this, however, went on inside Japan. Her foreign policy showed little of her resolution, for it had become an axiom of the Foreign Office after the Triple Intervention that Japan should avoid all international complications or adventures until she had acquired a sufficiency of armed might. During the Battle of the Concessions in 1898, therefore, Japan made no attempt to follow the example of the European Powers by extorting a lease of territory from China and contented herself with obtaining a guarantee of non-alienation to another Power for the province of Fukien opposite Formosa. Up to 1902 the limit of Japan's ambition was to prevent a Russian absorption of Korea; Russian power in Manchuria appeared in Tokyo, as in St. Petersburg, to be beyond the range of Japanese interference.

After the conclusion of the Anglo-Japanese

alliance, however, Japanese policy began to pay attention to Manchuria also—though even then Tokyo was ready to acquiesce in the Russian hold on Manchuria if Russia would strictly refrain from meddling in the affairs of Korea. But from 1895 Russia had taken advantage of the weakness of Korea and the anti-Japanese temper of the Seoul Court to extend her influence, and in 1903 the policing of a Russian timber concession on the Yalu river was made the excuse for the entry of Russian troops into Korea and the construction of a fort at Yongampo. Korea was the real bone of contention; the war of 1894 had been fought to decide whether China or Japan should dominate Korea, and the war of 1904 was to be fought to decide between a Japanese and a Russian ascendancy over the same country. But it had become clear that the only way to remove Russian power from Korea was to remove it also from the Chinese littoral of the Yellow Sea : in other words, to expel the Russians from Port Arthur. The Russo-Japanese war was fought *for* Korea, but *in* Manchuria, and it resulted not only in the annexation of Korea by Japan but also in the transfer to Japan of Russia's leasehold and railway zone rights in the most southerly of China's Manchurian provinces.

Success for Japan in the war depended on command of the sea. If the Japanese could gain and hold naval supremacy, they had the advantage for the campaign on land, because they would be near their homeland bases, whereas Russia would be fighting at the end of a single-track railway 5,000 miles from Moscow. On the other hand, Japan could do nothing on the mainland of Asia if the Russian navy were to render the sea unsafe for her transports. Russia's chance of winning the war lay in a bold naval initiative. She had only a part of her total navy in the Far East at the time of the outbreak of war, but a strength sufficient on paper to make the landing of big Japanese armies on the mainland an extremely risky enterprise. But the Russians showed a complete inability to use their fleet offensively; their only idea was to keep it 'in being' under the shelter of the Port Arthur shore batteries. They were matched against a supreme master of the art of naval warfare, and with 'a great sea-going squadron, manned by 15,000 of the best seamen of Russia, and representing in material alone a capital of thirty-two millions sterling' they were unable to sink one Japanese warship in battle or to prevent the enemy putting an army ashore within a few miles of their supposedly 'inaccessible stronghold'. The Japanese held command of the sea, while their land forces occupied Korea and Liao-tung, laying siege to Port Arthur and finally taking it, together with the residue of the Russian Pacific fleet shut up in its harbour.

After the capitulation of Port Arthur on January 2, 1905, the Japanese took the offensive against the Russian field army, which had now been brought up to something like equal numbers with its enemy, thanks to the great skill of the Russian Minister of Communications, Prince Khilkov, who performed miracles with the Trans-Siberian railway for the re-inforcement and supply of the forces in Manchuria. In the great battle of Mukden more than 300,000 men were engaged on either side—a breaking of all previous records for a single fight, small as it now seems in comparison with the grapple of armies in 1914–18. The Japanese victory in this battle estab-lished Japan once and for all as a Great Power, for the 'yellow pagans', as they were called in St. Petersburg, demonstrated an absolute military superiority over the European foe. 'Not once in all the long battle', wrote the Military Correspondent of *The Times*, 'did the Russian commander make any timely effort to control and dominate the situa-tion; from first to last he was as wax in the hands of the enemy. Troops, guns, priests, ikons, women—all became involved in one disorderly rout.'

Russia had still one card to play—her Baltic fleet, which was on paper not unequal to battle with the whole Japanese navy and might by a naval victory jeopardize all the hard-won Japanese gains on the mainland. The fleet was brought round Africa and through the Straits of Malacca into the China Seas, only to be attacked and destroyed by Togo in a vain attempt to slip through the Straits of Tsushima and reach Vladivostok (May 27–8).

It was the voyage of the Baltic fleet which nearly

brought about an extension of hostilities to Europe. By the terms of the Anglo-Japanese alliance England had been holding the ring for Japan ever since the struggle began. Russia's ally, France, showed no disposition to provoke a clash with England by any warlike action, though she stretched neutrality to its utmost limit by her 'boundless hospitality' to the Baltic fleet in the French harbours of Madagascar and Indo-China. The Anglo-French *entente* was a factor of international politics after the spring of 1904, and France was depending on British friendship for the accomplishment of her aims in Morocco. At the same time, she had no intention of renouncing her alliance with Russia, and as long as Anglo-Russian relations were strained her position was a difficult one, needing all the subtlety of M. Delcassé if France were not to end by giving offence to both sides. But France's dilemma was Germany's opportunity. Anglo-German relations were far from friendly and the German Government was no longer unwilling to take sides in the Anglo-Russian conflict. By drawing near to Russia and giving her support in the crisis of her fortunes Germany might supplant France as Russia's ally, France having so far compromised herself by her understanding with England. Germany gave Russia an assurance of security for her western frontiers and facilities for the coaling of her warships; the Kaiser encouraged the Tsar to believe that Russia 'must and will win'. On August 15, 1904, Lord Lansdowne warned the German Am-

bassador that if German breaches of neutrality involved Germany in war with Japan, England would,
on Japan's request, recognize the *casus foederis*.
Tension between England and Russia became acute
after the Dogger Bank incident of October 21 when
ships of the Russian Baltic fleet, passing through the
North Sea on their way to the Far East, fired on
trawlers from Hull in the belief that they were
Japanese torpedo-boats. A few days later the Kaiser
declared in a telegram to the Tsar:

'It is not impossible that the Japanese and British
Governments may launch joint protests against our coaling your ships, coupled with a summons to stop. The
result of such a threat of war would be the inability of
your fleet to proceed for want of fuel. This new danger
would have to be faced by Russia and Germany together,
who would both have to remind your ally France of her
obligations. It is out of the question that France would
try to shirk her duty.'

In reply the Tsar wired:

'The only way, as you say, would be that Germany,
Russia and France should at once unite upon arrangements to abolish English and Japanese insolence. . . .
This combination has often come to my mind; it will
mean peace and rest for the world.'

The proposed combination was, of course, simply
the old Dreibund which had acted against Japan in
1895. German diplomacy seemed to be on the verge
of a great success. Either there would be a united
front of the Dreibund against England or else France

would remain neutral in a line-up of Germany and Russia against England and Japan, in which case Germany would at least have separated Russia from France. But the German Government was not willing to risk war in order to prove its devotion to the Russian cause, and its failure to send colliers for the Baltic fleet farther than Madagascar greatly annoyed the Tsar.

After the destruction of the Baltic fleet in the Tsushima Straits on May 27–8 the war was virtually at an end, and the international storm-centre was no longer the travelling circus of Russian warships, but the question of Morocco, over which France and Germany came near to war in the first week of June. On this issue Russia had no cause to side with Germany or against England, and already with the decision of the conflict in the Far East a re-alignment of European Powers was beginning to take place. But the Kaiser was still hoping for a Russo-German alliance, and meeting the Tsar on his yacht at Bjorkö near Viborg, induced him to sign a treaty of alliance to which France was also to be invited to adhere. The Kaiser was delighted with his achievement, but he was wrong in supposing that Russia could be committed by the signature of her autocrat. The Tsar was bullied by the masterful Witte into repudiating the Treaty. It was in vain that the Kaiser pleaded that 'your ally notoriously left you in the lurch during the whole war, whereas Germany helped you in every way as far as she could without infringing the laws of neutrality'. Witte was made Prime Minister on October 20, as being the only man who could extricate the Russian state from its financial and moral collapse, and under him Russian foreign policy at once took a decidedly pro-French and anti-German turn.

The fact which the Kaiser failed to appreciate in what he regarded as his diplomatic triumph at Bjorkö was that Russia had been put back into Europe. The aim of German policy for over a decade had been to divert Russia from Europe to the Far East; as the Kaiser put it, 'the more the Russians get involved in Asia, the quieter they are in Europe'. But this purpose was finally frustrated by Togo's guns in May of 1905. Russia's Far Eastern adventure was finished—at any rate, as the controlling motive of her policy. In 1895 Russia had shifted her political axis from the Balkans to China; she was now to move it back again. In 1895 the Russian Ministers in Balkan capitals were instructed not to become involved in any intrigues which might embarrass the Government in St. Petersburg; three years after the battle of Tsushima, as soon as Russia had recovered a little from her post-war exhaustion and weakness, she was at odds with Austria in the Balkans, as she had been in the eighties. It was a disaster for Germany, who had rejected English overtures for an alliance because she would not oppose Russia, and now found Russia aligned against her.

There could only be Russo-German friendship as long as Russia's attention was diverted to the Far East; as soon as Russia's policy was again directed towards the Balkans, Russia was bound once more to clash with Austria, and therefore also with Germany. France had moreover consolidated her alliance by means of financial accommodation, and after the Russo-Japanese war Russia was in desperate need of funds. Prudence indicated the remoter and weaker rather than the nearer and stronger Power as the more desirable creditor. Desire to avoid dependence on a too neighbourly Germany and to retain a free hand for a Panslavist policy in the Balkans led Russia to choose Paris in preference to Berlin for her diplomatic *pied-à-terre* in Western Europe.

The Russo-German friendship was thus a thing of the past by the end of 1905. Its dissolution was the direct result of the Russo-Japanese war. From 1895 to 1905 it had more or less cancelled by a diplomatic cross-division the antagonism of the Franco-Russian and Austro-German groups which divided Continental Europe into two armed camps after the completion of the alliance-group system in 1893. Herein lies the significance of Far Eastern affairs for European politics during that decade. The Far Eastern situation imposed a regrouping of Powers which could never have been brought about if purely European issues had retained their primary importance for the relations of European states. The decade 1895–1905 was the imperialist epoch *par excellence* of modern European history. It was the time during which the more difficult problems of Europe were shelved and the policies of the Great Powers of Europe (except Austria) turned on disputes and stakes of interest in Asia and Africa. African questions assumed a great importance, but the threatened break-up of China provided the biggest problem of all. Political alignments in Europe were determined by relation to the Far Eastern Question more than by any other factor. In the succeeding period 1905–14 the Far East has very little relevance for European affairs; Morocco and the Balkans afford the occasions for international crises. The historical turning-point is the triumph of the Anglo-Japanese alliance over Russia in 1905. It is essential for the understanding of the diplomatic history of modern times to distinguish sharply between the periods 1895–1905 and 1905–14; unfortunately the historical perspective has been greatly distorted in the work of many historians by intensive study of 'war origins' (i.e. of the war of 1914) and over-emphasis on the lines of division between Triple Alliance and Triple Entente as they appear on the political map after 1907. In comparison with the clash of policies which led to the catastrophe of 1914 the stresses of 1895–1905 tend to seem unreal and unimportant, and what Bülow called 'the great Anglo-Russian conflict of interests', a mountain made out of a mole-hill. There is thus a general failure to appreciate fully the historical significance of Russia's Far Eastern empire-building from the Triple Intervention to the battle of Tsushima.

Because Russia was so disastrously beaten in the war of 1904–5 it is assumed that there never was any substance in 'the Russian danger', and that the idea of a Russian conquest of China was a lunatic's fantasy. But what was to have stopped Russia if Russian diplomacy had not committed the colossal folly of rejecting the repeated opportunities for a deal with Japan? If Russia had conceded an exclusive control of Korea to Japan, she would have met with no Japanese opposition to the accomplishment of her own far more extensive ambitions in China. It is clear that from 1895 to 1902 Japan was prepared to come to an agreement with Russia on these terms. Such an agreement would have left the Russians free to march to Peking and then to the Yangtse. If Russia had not driven Japan into the arms of England by refusing to meet her relatively trifling claim, where would England have found the 'Continental army to fight for her interests'? She could not have persuaded either France or Germany to oppose a Russian conquest of China, and she could not have defeated Russia's overland expansion merely by naval power. The Kaiser expressed his conviction to Sir Frank Lascelles in August 1898 that 'no one could stop Russia from marching with her army to Peking after she had made her preparations', and that 'England could never do anything from the water to a land Power such as Russia'. The Kaiser was

U

perfectly right. England would not have been able
to check Russia in the Far East without the Japanese
alliance, and she would never have obtained it but
for Russia's gross underestimate of Japan's strength
and consequent refusal to accept the excellent bargain she was offered. Even with the Japanese alliance the issue was not decided, for a war might go
against Japan, and England could not intervene
directly without the risk of bringing in France or
Germany or both. Japan did not fail when the test
came, but the issue was by no means such a foregone
conclusion as is now commonly supposed ; military
opinion in France and Germany was almost unanimous in expecting the victory of Russia. The actual
course of the struggle made havoc of pro-Russian
calculations, but there was at any rate one occasion
in the campaign when the Japanese were in danger
of a great disaster. They nearly lost the battle of
Heitoukai because they were less able than the Russians to stand the intense cold of a Manchurian
January, and their whole line might have been
crumpled up if the Russian high command had
taken full advantage of this fact.

Had Russia been willing to buy off Japan at the
very low price demanded or had she managed to win
the war of 1904, she would certainly have pushed
on her conquests by stages farther and farther into
China, with the result that the Anglo-Russian conflict would have been intensified, Russo-German
relations would have remained harmonious, and

France would have been driven to choose definitely between her entente with England and her alliance with Russia. What actually happened as a consequence of the war in Manchuria was that Germany and Russia parted company and that England and Russia were reconciled. The Anglo-Japanese alliance remained and was strengthened, but its point after 1907 was to be anti-German instead of anti-Russian.

The treaty of alliance between England and Japan was revised and renewed after Japan had finally won the war by the battle of Tsushima, but before peace had been concluded. The revision reflected the changed situation and the consciousness on the British side that the alliance was likely in future to be more necessary for England than for Japan. There was now no considerable threat to Japan's security, for it was extremely improbable that Russia, after her bitter experience, would attempt to upset the new order of things in the Far East. England, however, apprehended new dangers for herself. Russia, after a pause for internal reconstruction, might renew her movement of expansion in Asia, no longer towards China but towards India; or again, Germany might take advantage of Russia's temporary disablement to attack France in a war which could hardly fail to involve England. For either of these contingencies the Japanese alliance would be of very great value to England; against Russia, because Japan could relieve pressure in Central Asia by a threat to

Vladivostok, and against Germany, because her navy
could protect British shipping in the Pacific against
commerce-raiders and thus render possible a greater
concentration of the British fleet in home waters. In
the new treaty the scope of the alliance was extended
to embrace India, and Japan recognized England's
right 'to take such measures in the proximity of that
frontier as she may find necessary for safeguarding
her Indian possessions'. At the same time the alliance was made operative if either signatory should
be attacked by a single Power instead of only in case
of attack by two or more, as in the original treaty.
For this extension of her liabilities Japan naturally
exacted her price, and her price was a free hand in
Korea. According to the new treaty:

'Japan possessing paramount political, military and
economic interests in Korea, Great Britain recognizes
her right to take such measures of guidance, control and
protection in Korea as she may deem necessary, provided
that they are not contrary to the principle of equal
opportunities for the commerce and industry of all
nations.'

This formula was sufficient to cover the political
absorption and eventual annexation of Korea by
Japan.

Less than a month after the renewal of the Anglo-
Japanese alliance in its new form, the Russo-Japanese
war was formally concluded by a treaty signed at
Portsmouth, New Hampshire, the United States
having acted as mediator between the belligerents.

Russia ceded to Japan the southern half of Sakhalin, undertook to evacuate Manchuria except for a limited force of railway guards, surrendered the Kwantung Leased Territory with the towns of Port Arthur and Dalny and the railway as far north as Changchun, and recognized Japanese supremacy in Korea. The peace treaty was a great disappointment to the Japanese public, which had been led to expect an indemnity from Russia, and the popular displeasure expressed itself in serious rioting in Tokyo. But the Japanese Government had been wise in not pressing its vanquished enemy too hard. Japan had achieved the main objective of her policy—the exclusion of Russian power from Korea and southern Manchuria—without closing the door to a *rapprochement* with Russia after a short lapse of time. With no indemnity or 'reparations' burden to prolong bitter feeling for years to come, Russia and Japan were soon able to get together in an amicable partnership. The rulers of Russia had learnt their lesson. As Mr. P. Joseph admirably puts it,[1] 'It took the Russo-Japanese War to convince Russia that they [Russia and Japan] were natural allies.'

The position of China in relation to the Treaty of Portsmouth was a peculiar one. The war had been waged on Chinese territory, but China had been officially neutral and had remained a mere passive spectator of the military operations. Before the outbreak of war Manchuria was already lost to China,

[1] *Foreign Diplomacy in China 1894–1900*, p. 143.

for all three provinces—except for the area between Shanhaikwan and the Liao river—were occupied by the Russians, and it was clear that nothing but force would ever remove them. Japan fought nominally to compel Russia to evacuate Manchuria, or in other words, to restore it to Chinese sovereignty. But she did not in fact pour out blood and treasure in order to do for China what China could not do for herself. The Japanese Army which had overrun southern Manchuria in 1894 and again in 1904, regarded it as a Japanese possession by right of conquest, and if the peace treaty of 1905 could have been made solely by negotiation between Russia and Japan, it is probable that Manchuria would have been in some way partitioned between the belligerents. Japan would not have objected to a Russian annexation of the north, if she could have taken the south, of Manchuria. But Japan was deprived of any such 'fruits of victory' just as effectively as she had been in 1895, though in a much less obvious way. She was not made this time to disgorge territory ceded to her or threatened with violent intervention. She was merely held to her professed war aims by the nations on whom she was financially dependent. The Anglo-Japanese alliance guaranteed 'the independence and integrity of the Chinese Empire', and the revision of the alliance treaty in 1905 did not modify this principle, as it did the original provision with regard to Korea. The American Government was even more strongly opposed to any settlement of the Russo-

Japanese war at the expense of China. Japan, bled white financially by the war, was in no position to resist Anglo-American insistence on the restoration of Chinese sovereignty in Manchuria, and had to be content with her paramountcy in Korea. So it came about that China, without firing a single shot in the war, was the principal gainer by its result as far as Manchuria was concerned. Russia withdrew her troops and renounced all rights 'in impairment of Chinese sovereignty'. Only the Kwantung Leased Territory and part of the Russian-built railway from Harbin to Port Arthur were 'transferred and assigned' to Japan, and this was made subject to China's consent. China was at length induced to give her consent, but showed great reluctance, and it was clear before the end of the year that there was going to be endless trouble and controversy between China and Japan over the transferred rights in Manchuria. The wrangling was to go on continuously for twenty-six years until the Japanese Army marched to the Great Wall and formally separated Manchuria from China as the 'independent' state of Manchukuo. The crisis of 1931 was due to the increasingly effective endeavour of China to assert her sovereignty over Manchuria, in fact as well as in name, and the economic interests involved provide a sufficient explanation for the sharpness of the conflict which arose.

The extraordinary intensity of feeling provoked in Japan on the Manchurian issue cannot be fully understood except by reference to the Japanese view of the implications of the Portsmouth Treaty. The Japanese have always held that the Chinese reaped where they had not sown by a treaty which restored to them three provinces ransomed at the cost of 120,000 Japanese lives, and that their sovereignty was limited by an obligation to accord a privileged status to Japanese interests. The Chinese have never admitted any such obligation, holding that Manchuria always legally belonged to them and that they received no more than what was due to them in the settlement of 1905.

The idea that South Manchuria should have been part of the spoils of war was very widespread in Japan in 1906, and was extremely embarrassing to the first Saionji Cabinet which was trying faithfully to carry out the treaty provisions. Count Hayashi, who had negotiated the Anglo-Japanese alliance and was Foreign Minister in this Cabinet, defended himself after its fall in an apologia which throws a vivid light on contemporary controversy.

'The principal point', he writes, 'on which the late Cabinet was attacked was that we had spent in Manchuria several hundred millions of yen and 100,000 lives in order to win our rights and privileges in that country; they say we ought not, therefore, to be slack in our policy in Manchuria. . . . To say that we fought for China is rather stretching the truth. There may be some truth in the statement, but to expect other people to believe it is like trying "to steal a bell by shutting one's own ears". Although we drove the Russians away we have come in their stead, so, looked at from the Chinese point of view,

we may be likened to "the wolf that follows the tiger"....
It is easy to imagine how boastful and arrogant our
soldiers were after the Russo-Japanese War. By what
they did there [in Manchuria] after the war we have not
only lost the goodwill of the Chinese, but have incurred
the adverse criticism of Europeans and Americans.'

Faced with Chinese hostility, kept under censorious
observation by British and American commercial interests, and harassed in domestic politics by military
chauvinists who urged a bold policy of acquisition
in Manchuria, the Japanese Government hastened
to establish a working partnership with its late enemy
in arms. Japan had acquired a share in the system
of railway zone rights, forming an *imperium in imperio*,
created by the Russians in Manchuria, and the two
Powers recently at war had now a common interest
to defend both against China and against foreign in-
terlopers. Russia also felt the need for an understanding, and the Motono-Isvolsky Agreement, signed on
July 30, 1907, provided the basis of a Russo-Japanese
entente. The signatories described themselves as
'wishing to remove for the future every cause of mis-
understanding in the relations of the two Empires',
and agreed to respect 'all the rights accruing to one
and the other Party from the treaties, conventions and
contracts in force between them and China'. So far
the published version; secret clauses partitioned Manchuria into Russian and Japanese spheres of influence.
Seven weeks before this convention with Russia Japan
had concluded an agreement with France in which

the two states promised mutual support for assuring peace and security in 'regions of the Chinese Empire adjacent to the territories where they have rights of sovereignty, protection or occupation'—in other words recognition for a French sphere in Kwangsi and Yunnan, and a Japanese sphere in South Manchuria.

Japan was thus reconciled, and more than reconciled, with France and Russia, but this did not mean any weakening of the Anglo-Japanese alliance. On the contrary, the liquidation of the Russo-Japanese conflict was most welcome to England, who was herself joining hands with Russia. The Russo-Japanese deal over Manchuria was inevitably adverse to certain British business concerns intending to operate in Manchuria, but it was regarded in London as an essential element politically in the new grouping of Powers against Germany, which England's fear of Germany's increasing navy was leading her to promote. Fear of Germany had now definitely replaced fear of Russia as the dominant motive of British foreign policy. Russia's navy had been nearly wiped out in the war with Japan and would take many years to restore. Russian military power, deprived of its base in South Manchuria, could no longer threaten Peking, and had in any case been proved by the ordeal of war to be less formidable than had been hitherto supposed.

The fear that Russia, headed off from China, would concentrate attention on Afghanistan had proved groundless. It was clear by 1907 that for the next few years the main pressure of Russian policy was going to be in Europe and not in Asia. 'The great Anglo-Russian conflict of interests' was therefore at an end. But Anglo-German tension arising out of naval rivalry grew more and more acute, and England, without entering into any definite alliance, drew closer to the Franco-Russian camp. The Anglo-French entente of 1904 now had its natural sequel in an Anglo-Russian entente with a settlement of outstanding differences in regard to Persia, Afghanistan, and Tibet. The three agreements of 1907—Japan and France (June 10), Japan and Russia (July 30), and England and Russia (August 31)—meant that the Franco-Russian and Anglo-Japanese alliances were now linked together in a Four-Power group isolating Germany in Far Eastern affairs.

IX

THE EVICTION OF GERMANY

WHEN Japan applied at Peking for Chinese consent to the transfer of the leases surrendered by Russia, she also obtained from China an undertaking which was to be the juridical foundation of her claim to an exclusive economic sphere in South Manchuria. The Chinese Government agreed by a declaration not embodied in the formal treaty but entered in the minutes of the Conference, 'not to construct, prior to the recovery by them of the said railway [Changchun to Port Arthur], any line in the neighbourhood of and parallel to that railway, or any branch line which would be prejudicial to its interests'.

The principle laid down was clear enough, but the vague drafting of the clause left plenty of room for differences in interpretation. The Japanese soon showed that they interpreted it in the widest sense and regarded it as giving them a monopoly of railway construction in South Manchuria. This claim ran counter to the Chinese intention of building new railways in Manchuria with capital borrowed from nations other than Russia and Japan and of making them subject to real Chinese control—from which the Chinese Eastern system by the terms of the original contract was virtually immune. It was recognized at Peking that the withdrawal of Russian and Japanese troops from Manchuria and the restoration of Chinese authority in the civil administration did not mean a full recovery of sovereignty in the three provinces as long as an unrivalled economic power remained in the hands of the Russian and Japanese railways. To have effective control of Manchuria China must have her own railway system and become independent of the existing lines. The resistance of Japan to Chinese enterprises undertaken with this end in view led to a series of conflicts with far-reaching diplomatic repercussions.

In the months immediately following the close of the Russo-Japanese war there was a tendency in Japan to regard the transferred railway titles in South Manchuria as something of a white elephant, a property acquired in order to cut off Russian access to the Yellow Sea rather than for its own sake. Japan was distressed financially after a struggle which she had only been able to carry on by heavy borrowing abroad, and it seemed unlikely that the railways could be made profitable without a large outlay of capital; tracks and plant had deteriorated with war-time wear and tear. Under the influence of such considerations, the Japanese Prime Minister, Count Katsura, entered into a provisional agreement with the American railway magnate Harriman for the joint ownership of the transferred railways and mines in Manchuria by the Japanese Government and an American syndicate. This scheme was brought to nothing by the intervention of the Foreign

Minister, Baron Komura, who had gone to America for the negotiation of the peace treaty and had not returned to Japan when the Katsura-Harriman conversations took place. Komura maintained that the transferred rights were of the greatest importance both economically and politically, and must be retained under Japanese control. This view gained ground rapidly and the new trend of opinion led to the formation in the summer of 1906 of the famous S.M.R. (South Manchuria Railway) Company to take over and work the railways and associated concerns. Half the capital was provided by the Government, and the other half raised by subscription limited to Chinese and Japanese nationals. The Chinese would not subscribe, and the shares were all taken up in Japan. Ultimate control rested in the hands of the Japanese Government, and the Presidency of the Company became a very important political appointment. The original articles of incorporation fixed the Company's capital at 200 million yen. Capitalization was increased to 440 million in 1920 and the figure had risen to 800 million by 1935. This great semi-governmental concern has been ever since its creation at once an instrument of Japanese national policy and a major factor in the determination of that policy.

The organization of Japan's S.M.R. was strikingly similar in type to that of Russia's C.E.R. (Chinese Eastern Railway), and this was a natural result of the transfer to Japan of rights which had been bound

up with the C.E.R. system. The C.E.R. had been
Witte's instrument for the politico-economic penetration of Manchuria, 'conquest by railway and bank'
as it was called, and its administrative and police
powers were far too extensive to be without political
significance. The Japanese were the heirs of this
system in the area of cession ; they did not originate
it. They simply took over the apparatus of Russian
imperialism.

The first trial of strength in Manchuria after the
Russo-Japanese war took place towards the end of
1907 when the Chinese Government assigned a concession to a British firm for the construction of a
railway from Hsinmintun to Fakumen. Japan protested on the ground that the concession was in vio-
lation of China's undertaking not to build lines
'parallel' to the S.M.R. China took no notice at first
of the Japanese veto, but ceased to press the matter
and finally backed out of the enterprise after the
Japanese objection had been endorsed by the British
Foreign Office in spite of the fact that a British firm
was involved. The episode revealed a divergence,
hitherto rare in British Far Eastern policy, between
British political and commercial interest. The aim
of this policy was no longer simply to maintain the
open door and see that no British subject received
less than his rights in business transactions. The im-
perious political need for confirming alliances and
ententes and not offending countries which might
conceivably decide to sail on a pro-German course

was now decisive for the official attitude on such questions as the Fakumen concession. London was not going to hazard the Japanese alliance for the right of Messrs. Pauling & Co. to lay forty-seven miles of railway. The Japanese objection was allowed.

The U.S.A., however, was not affected by the motives of expediency which now determined British policy, and American financiers were next involved in an attack on the Manchurian enclosures. Harriman, whose scheme for operating the South Manchuria lines had been frustrated by Japanese nationalism, had worked out new plans in which he interested the American State Department. A preliminary concession was secured for a railway from Chinchow to Aigun, that is, right through Manchuria from the Pechihli Gulf to the Amur. With this as a bargaining lever Secretary Knox circularized late in 1909 a proposal for the neutralization of the Manchurian railways, which were to be bought up and operated by an international syndicate. The Chinchow-Aigun railway was to be built if the neutralization plan fell through. The American proposals had little chance of success even with the most skilful diplomatic handling, but whatever chance they might have had was ruined by clumsy presentation. The American Ambassador in Tokyo misrepresented the British attitude to the proposals, and the American communication to St. Petersburg suppressed part of the plan as revealed to other

Governments. As a result of these subterfuges Russia and Japan were convinced that they had to deal with a diplomatic initiative of more than usual dishonesty, and made common cause in opposition to the scheme—which was in any case detrimental to their interests. A new Russo-Japanese agreement was concluded in July 1910, which not only confirmed the sphere arrangements of 1907, but provided for consultation and mutual support in defence of these interests. England gave a cautious but firm support to Russia and Japan, and Knox was rebuffed. Not only was the neutralization scheme turned down, but pressure was put on China not to sign the final agreement for the Chinchow-Aigun railway, and Peking yielded to the veto.

The main result of the ill-considered American intervention was to drive Japan and Russia towards more extreme courses and to inflame the chauvinist spirit in both countries. Japan asserted herself by the outright annexation of Korea. The relation of 'paramount political, military, and economic interests' had for some time past been found unsatisfactory; a revolt in Korea had given great trouble and the assassination of Ito by a Korean at Harbin in October 1909 exasperated Japanese government circles. There was a growing demand for annexation, and when it appeared that the U.S.A. was trying to drive a wedge of internationalism into Japan's quasi-colonial domain on the Continent, it was felt that the ambiguity of Korea's status must not be allowed to continue. A Treaty of Annexation was signed on August 22, 1910, and the Korean 'Emperor'[1] surrendered his sovereignty, already attenuated to vanishing-point. Foreign Powers which had formerly had Legations in Seoul had already withdrawn them in view of the Korean-Japanese Protocol of 1905 which gave Japan control of Korea's foreign relations. The annexation, therefore, produced no international complications of an official kind, but there was much outcry of unofficial opinion in the United States where a Korean nationalist propaganda had had considerable effect.

Russia in the same year contemplated the annexation in full sovereignty of North Manchuria so as to bring the whole Chita-Harbin-Vladivostok line of railway within Russian territory. The suggestion of a Sino-American line up to the Amur had been a great shock to Russian nerves. At a ministerial council in December the Minister of War demanded the annexation, but Sazonov, now Foreign Minister, advised caution, as 'America, England, perhaps even Japan, would oppose our plans and we could expect no support from any quarter whatever'. The biting-off of a Chinese province in this way was indeed a much more serious matter for international politics than the swallowing whole of a small kingdom which had already ceased to have any foreign relations.

---

[1] The king of Korea took the title of 'Emperor' in 1896. The change was meant to signify that Korea was no longer a tributary of China, but a state on an equality with China and Japan.

The council decided that it 'regards annexation as dangerous at the present moment, but is of opinion that the trend of events may force Russia to this step', and meanwhile, 'our stipulated privileges in North Manchuria must be maintained in full, to permit, eventually, an annexation at some future date'.

Russia did not annex North Manchuria, but the Russo-Japanese combine tightened up its unofficial supremacy in the three provinces after the failure of the American Government to gain acceptance for the railway neutralization scheme. Russia and Japan respected each other's spheres and united to maintain them against third parties—including China. Nor did the Russo-Japanese sphere-delimiting agreements apply only to Manchuria; they embraced all the territories of the Chinese empire outside the Great Wall—that is to say, Manchuria, Mongolia, and Eastern Turkestan or Sinkiang. Russia recognized Japan's sphere as including not only South Manchuria, but also Inner (South) Mongolia, while Japan gave corresponding recognition to a Russian sphere covering North Manchuria, Outer (North) Mongolia, and 'West China'. The term 'West China' was conveniently vague; it certainly meant in the first place Sinkiang, but it could always be stretched to take in also Kansu and Shensi which were provinces of China Proper.[1] The idea of invading China

[1] The ambiguity in the geographical extension of the name 'China' has been a frequent cause of misunderstandings and disputes. 'China'

from the north-west was no part of Russia's immediate political programme, but it was kept in mind as a possibility for the future, and we have a record of a Russian plan of expansion in this quarter which is especially interesting to-day in view of the present Soviet Russian ascendancy in Sinkiang.

Early in 1898, after a Russian naval squadron had anchored off Port Arthur, but before the place had been definitely occupied, the British Government made an attempt to arrive at a friendly understanding with Russia, and the British Ambassador in St. Petersburg was instructed to discover as far as he could what were the ultimate aims of the Russians in the Far East. The Ambassador sent in a report of his interview with Witte in which the latter had suggested a partition of the Chinese empire into Russian and British spheres. 'Producing from a carefully locked desk a map of China, the Minister [Witte] proceeded to draw his hand over the provinces of Chihli, Shansi, Shensi, and Kansu, and said that sooner or later Russia would probably absorb all this territory.' He went on to explain that it was planned to construct a branch line of the Siberian railway to Lanchow, the provincial capital of Kansu on the upper course of the Yellow River, and declared that he already had detailed technical reports on the project. This line, however, has never yet been

could mean (1) the whole Chinese (Manchu dynastic) empire or (2) China Proper, which was formerly distinguished from the four dependencies of Manchuria, Mongolia, Sinkiang, and Tibet.

built. The economic objection to it, as to any railway entering China from the north or north-west,
was decisive. The line would have to cross some
part of the Taklamakan-Gobi desert belt, which
would make it costly to construct and unprofitable
to operate. The railway approach to China from
the north-east, through Manchuria, was economically a much sounder proposition; there was no desert,
but a country with vast possibilities of commercial
development and close connexions with ports on the
Japan and Yellow Seas. The scheme for a line to
Lanchow was therefore abandoned, but it was not
forgotten, and after the Russo-Japanese war there
was some consolation for the failure of Russia's Manchurian policy in the thought of a possible new approach to China in a quarter where Russia would
not have to cross swords with Japan. Actually,
Russia was incapable of undertaking such an enterprise after 1905, because she was financially exhausted and was only restored by French loans which
carried with them the condition that she should conserve her strength for European politics and not dissipate it in new Asiatic adventures. Nevertheless, the
Lanchow railway was an idea which might some day
become a reality, and the way for it was kept open
by the claim to a sphere of influence in West China.

Apart from the scheme for reaching China Proper
from the north-west, the Russian sphere included
practically all Chinese territory north of the so-called
Kuropatkin Line, a straight line drawn from the Khan

Tengri range of the T'ien-shan mountains to Vladivostok—roughly the forty-third parallel of latitude.
The political strategists of St. Petersburg desired to
make this line the frontier of Russia-in-Asia, thereby approximately halving the length of the existing
Russo-Chinese border, which ran up to the Sayan
mountains and the great northern bend of the Amur.
If Tsarist Russia had survived the Great War, a
formal redrawing of the map in this way would probably have taken place at an early date.

An important step towards the goal was taken in
1912 when the Mongols revolted against China after
the abdication of the Manchu dynasty. The revolutionary movement which broke out in the autumn
of 1911 had resulted in the foundation of a 'Republic of China', which adopted instead of the dragon
flag of the old empire a banner of five bars representing the five nationalities which were now to
dwell together in republican amity—the Chinese, the
Manchus, the Mongols, the Mohammedans,[1] and the
Tibetans. Neither the Tibetans nor the Mongols, however, had any intention of belonging to the new state
and they took advantage of the confusion following
on the Revolution to make themselves independent.
The Mongols in particular were hostile to the Republic. Their tribal princes reckoned themselves vassals of the Manchu dynasty and did not allow that
they owed any allegiance to China as such, since

[1] Divided into Chinese-speaking (Tungans) and Turki-speaking
(Kashgaris, Kirghiz, &c.).

the Mongols had not been subdued by the Chinese but had, on the contrary, been partners with the Manchus in the conquest of China. For Europeans the Manchu empire was the Chinese empire, but for the Mongols it was always a Manchu ascendancy which had in its decline been perverted into the service of purely Chinese interests. The estrangement of the dynasty from its Manchu-Mongol national origins and its promotion of Chinese immigration into Manchuria and Mongolia had already strained the loyalty of the Mongol tribes. Originally Manchuria and Mongolia had been kept quite separate from China Proper within the framework of the Manchu empire, and the Chinese had been forbidden to settle north of the Great Wall except in areas which they already inhabited, but the rule had gradually been relaxed, partly owing to Chinese pressure and partly owing to the Peking Government's desire to forestall Russian colonization in the northern territories of the empire.

The process of Chinese colonization in Manchuria had been facilitated by the Liao-Sungari-Amur system of water-ways and, after 1896, by the Russian railway building. There was no resistance from the Manchus, who had been dispersed from their original country by their empire-making, and who, having no strongly differentiated culture of their own, were susceptible to the assimilating influences of China. Thus the 'land of the Manchus' became ethnically a part of China.

In Mongolia, on the other hand, and in those parts of Manchuria where the population was Mongol, the intrusion of Chinese colonists only created an acute nationality problem. Colonization was not aided by rivers and railways west of Manchuria, and the Gobi desert dividing Outer from Inner Mongolia was an effective barrier to Chinese peasant emigration. Chinese peasant settlement was therefore confined to Inner Mongolia south of the desert, but Chinese traders and money-lenders were active also in Outer Mongolia. The Mongols were nowhere assimilated by the Chinese; their specialized pastoral-nomadic way of life and their national Lama-Buddhist religion with its elaborate ecclesiastical organization gave them a strong national consciousness, though politically they were divided into ten 'leagues' (*chiguglan*) subdivided into a large number of 'banners' (*hoshun*) under hereditary princes (*jassak*). Encroachments of Chinese agriculture on the less arid sections of the Mongols' pasture lands and impoverishment due to Chinese usury produced a bitter anti-Chinese sentiment among the Mongols which manifested itself in a general insurrection in 1912. Chinese forces, now in the service of the Republic, held Inner Mongolia for China, but in Outer Mongolia the revolt was successful, and Mongolian independence under the Khutukhtu or Living Buddha, the head of the Mongol Lama-Buddhist Church, was proclaimed in Urga by a council of princes. Russia now warned China that any attempt

THE MONGOLIAN STEPPE

to reconquer Outer Mongolia would be met by Russian intervention, and compelled the Peking Government to recognize the Urga administration as an autonomous state under Chinese suzerainty. China was henceforth to be represented at Urga by a Resident, but the country became to all intents and purposes a Russian protectorate, as the Mongols depended on Russia for their security against Chinese domination and granted all kinds of economic privileges as the price of her support.

The creation of a Russian-protected Mongol state was, however, only one of the important consequences of the Chinese Revolution of 1911, and it was regarded as a matter between China and Russia, no other Power at that time claiming to have an interest in Outer Mongolia. Of far greater international significance was the insolvency of the Chinese state which was aggravated by the revolutionary convulsion. Financially China was in a desperate position as a result of the utter inadequacy of the revenues available for the purposes of the central government. Since 1900 there had been an effort at modernization more serious than any of the reform experiments of the nineteenth century. The disastrous failure of the Boxer 'war against the world' had left traditionalism hopelessly discredited, and even the Empress-Dowager gave her consent to a programme of far-reaching reforms. But for these reforms money was needed, and the raising of adequate revenue meant a radical alteration of the whole political system. The old method whereby the provincial authorities collected taxes and remitted certain sums to Peking had worked well enough in the old days of seclusion, but it could not sustain the expenditure of a modern national state. On the other hand a thorough-going centralization and reform of the fiscal apparatus would range against the central government both the sentiments of provincial particularism and countless vested interests of corruption.

The Manchu Court, only too well aware of the rottenness and unpopularity of the régime, feared to provoke such a struggle. The revenues of the Maritime Customs were paid direct to Peking, but the state's foreign obligations were a first charge on them, and neither they nor other dues levied on foreign trade could be increased because the tariff rates had been fixed by treaty. But what the central government could do was to go on borrowing abroad, because the system of providing security by means of foreign control of Chinese revenues meant that China's credit abroad stood far higher than the general state of the country's finances would warrant. The foreign creditor would get paid if every official, soldier, and contractor in China went without his money; he was therefore prepared to lend. But inasmuch as the security for loans to China involved a measure of political domination and was further complicated by the question of spheres of influence, financial transactions with the Middle Kingdom were no business for unaided private enterprise but were matters of concern to governments, to be supervised and encouraged or restricted in accordance with political aims. The real trouble began when a number of English, American, French, and German banks combined in 1910 in a 'Four Power Group' for supplying credits to China. A sum of money advanced by this group was to be used 'for the promotion and extension of industrial enterprises in the three Manchurian provinces', and this at once brought Russia and Japan on the scene with claims to enter the Consortium on the ground of their 'special interests' in the region affected, in spite of the fact that both of them were debtor nations and ill qualified to be represented in a money-lenders' association. But banking business was not to be separated from political considerations which took into account every important factor in the world situation. The Four Power banking Consortium of England, America, France, and Germany overlapped with the Four Power political combine of England, France, Russia, and Japan. England and France were common to both groups and did not dare to turn a deaf ear to the pleas and protests of their political allies. Prolonged negotiations took place, and in the end the Consortium was enlarged to take in Russia and Japan, who were thus enabled to obstruct any loan which might be used for the weakening of their supremacies in Manchuria and Mongolia.

Meanwhile the Manchu dynasty collapsed and the Chinese Republic was set up in its stead. The Peking

Government having raised a loan from the Four Power Consortium for railway construction in central China came into conflict with the interests of a private railway company in the province of Szechwan. The shareholders were local gentry, and, making the matter an issue between province and central power, they started an armed insurrection. The revolt spread down the Yangtse and was transformed into a republican movement under Cantonese leadership. All China south of Yangtse passed into the hands of the rebels, but a powerful Northern army loyal to the monarchy barred the way to Peking. There was no sign of a quick military decision of the civil war, but money power turned the scales. The republican cause was financed by the radically inclined bourgeoisie of Canton and Shanghai as well as by the wealthy Chinese communities (almost entirely of Kwangtung and Fukien origin) in Hong Kong, Singapore, Batavia, San Francisco, and elsewhere abroad. The Peking Government, on the other hand, relied on foreign credits for money to pay its troops. But the Consortium was paralysed by the diplomatic wrangle arising out of the attempt of Russia and Japan to force their way in, and until a settlement had been reached, the bankers were unwilling to enter on any large commitments. Also, the British commercial interests in the southern ports, threatened with boycott by the pro-republican guilds, favoured 'non-intervention'. The Manchu monarchy was unable to raise money, and an edict of abdication was issued on behalf of the seven-year-old Emperor, declaring that 'it is clear that the minds of the majority of the people are favourable to the establishment of a republican form of government. . . . The universal desire clearly expresses the will of Heaven, and it is not for us to oppose the desires and incur the disapproval of the millions of the people merely for the sake of the privileges and powers of a single House.'

The dynasty which had ruled China for 268 years was thus removed, and the republicans entered into the inheritance of an empty treasury and an unpaid army. The looting of Peking by mutinous troops was an event of unhappy augury for the new régime. It was now the Republic's turn to seek a foreign loan, and the Consortium was found to be again ready to do business, the conflict of the Powers having been settled by the inclusion of Japan and Russia in the Consortium, 'special interests' and all. A 'reorganization loan' was arranged with the Consortium. But who was to have the power of the purse in the new China? As long as China had been a dynastic autocracy there had been no doubt as to the authority with whom the bankers had to deal. Now it was not so clear. By a provisional constitution drawn up under the influence of American republican principles there was to be a parliament and a President. The parliament, when elected, contained a majority of members of the newly formed Kuomintang party led by the doctrinaire republican

Sun Yat-sen, but the President was Yuan Shih-k'ai, who had been the favourite minister of the Empress-Dowager Tze Hsi after 1900, had been dismissed from office after her death in 1908, and had been recalled to save the dynasty in 1911. He was anything but a republican, but he was supported by a powerful body of troops, and was too strong to be eliminated. The republicans therefore sought to capture him for the new régime and to unify the country by electing him to the Presidency, Sun Yatsen, who had been elected while the civil war was in progress, resigning in order to make way for him. Such a compromise could not be the basis of a stable government, and as soon as the new parliament was elected the struggle began. The Kuomintang politicians were already aware of the dangers of the American constitutional model in Chinese conditions, and aimed at reducing the President to a mere figurehead, as in the French republic; they were supported by certain generals who hoped to upset Yuan and make themselves independent in their provincial commands. Yuan, for his part, was determined to govern autocratically by means of the army and to get rid of the parliament if it tried to thwart him; for this he needed the disposal of the 'reorganization loan'.

The foreign Powers with commercial interests in China desired to see the country under the rule of a 'strong man'. They were alarmed at the prevailing disorder and the prospect of a period of anarchy and

civil wars with interruption of trade, decline of the
Customs revenues, on which loans were secured, and
perhaps a renewal of anti-foreign riots and massacres.
The diplomats and bankers decided to back Yuan,
who had been by far the most eminent of Chinese
statesmen since the death of Li Hung-chang and was
undoubtedly a 'strong man'. The exception to the
general agreement was Japan, for whom he was
altogether too much of a strong man; as Chinese
Resident in Seoul he had thwarted Japanese policy
in Korea for a decade, and the Tokyo Foreign Office
was only too well aware that his great ability went
with a strongly anti-Japanese conception of foreign
policy. However, Japan's apprehensions could not
deflect the general will of the Consortium, which
was to provide Yuan with funds.

Prolonged negotiations took place on the question
of security for the loan, the Maritime Customs being
no longer regarded as adequate to sustain the burden
of China's debt. The new loan was secured by a lien
on other revenues, notably the salt monopoly, and
these were to be brought under foreign administrative supervision. Disputes over the appointments of
financial advisers and political manœuvres within
the Consortium led to the withdrawal of the U.S.A.,
and the loan agreement (for £25 millions) was
finally concluded in April 1913 by the banks of the
remaining five states.

Yuan now had his money, and proceeded to defy
the Kuomintang. Sun Yat-sen led a rebellion against

him with the aid of malcontent generals, but it was easily suppressed and Sun fled to Japan. In the autumn Yuan outlawed the Kuomintang and abolished the parliament. He now governed with the aid of a carefully packed Council of State, and in May 1914 he promulgated a new constitution by virtue of which he assumed the position of dictator; it was enacted that the President was to hold office for ten years and to be re-eligible. Yuan's martinet authority had restored discipline in the army and order in the country at large, and it appeared that China was about to enter on a period of stronger and more efficient government than she had known for more than a century. As President of the Republic, Yuan ruled China as he had virtually ruled it from 1901 to 1908, but with the difference that he was no longer hampered by the intrigues of the Manchu Court. Already he was beginning to consider the idea of restoring the monarchy with himself as Emperor.

The undoing of Yuan Shih-k'ai was the assassination of the Archduke Ferdinand at Sarajevo on June 28 of 1914. Within six weeks the four European Powers of the Consortium, England, France, Germany, and Russia, were involved in a life-and-death struggle in their own continent, and Yuan suddenly found himself left alone, face to face with a hostile Japan.

The first Far Eastern consequence of the outbreak of war in Europe was the elimination of Germany; the second was the disintegration of China. Japan adhered to her alliance with England and her semi-alliance with Russia, in spite of the propaganda of a pro-German clique in the army which expected a German victory in Europe. War was declared against Germany on August 23, and a Japanese expeditionary force, joined by a detachment of British troops, was sent against Tsingtao, the fortified port of the German Kiaochow Leased Territory. The place was garrisoned by 13,000 German troops, and was potentially of great strategic value to Germany as a base for the raiding of Allied maritime commerce. It proved, however, a mere hostage to fortune, for it only stood a very short siege and could give no support to Admiral von Spee's cruiser squadron which was at large in the Pacific. The first landing of the Japanese expedition was made outside the German leased zone, with Chinese permission, and Tsingtao was invested by land and sea. It surrendered on November 7. Germany's China stronghold thus followed Russia's into the hands of the Japanese, and the flag of the Rising Sun waved over both the harbours where the Kaiser had seen 'St. George and St. Michael shielding the Holy Cross in the Far East and guarding the gates to the continent of Asia'.

The Japanese navy assisted the British in chasing von Spee's squadron out of the Pacific and occupied the islands belonging to Germany north of the Equator. These islands, some three thousand in number and most of them uninhabited, composed the

Marshall, Pelew, Caroline, and Marianne groups; they had belonged to Spain as part of her Philippines domain before 1898 and had been sold to Germany when the Philippines were ceded to the U.S.A. Meanwhile Australian and New Zealand forces had occupied German New Guinea and Samoa, so that Germany's colonial empire in the Pacific was wiped out.

Japan declined to accede to Allied requests for military aid in Europe and took no further direct part in the war against Germany, except to send a number of destroyers to the Mediterranean for convoy work against German submarines. This was not in itself a major operation, but it was of great value to the European Allies, because the submarine campaign was a serious menace and they could ill afford to spare warships for convoys. The severe strain which the third year of the war imposed on them enabled Japan to obtain assurances of support at the post-war peace conference for a claim to the cession of the German rights in Shantung and the Pacific islands north of the Equator. England gave this pledge in an exchange of notes on February 16, 1917, and France and Russia followed suit a little later; it was understood that the Japanese anti-submarine campaign was conditional on the promises with regard to Shantung and the islands.

Japan had meanwhile obtained the consent of China to the transfer by one of the treaties arising out of the 'Twenty-one Demands'. Immediately after the Japanese capture of Tsingtao China had demanded the evacuation of the Japanese forces and the return of the leased territory to Chinese administration, even putting in a claim for damages on account of military operations outside the leased zone. The Japanese, however, were not at all prepared to hand over the conquered territory to China, and demanded that China should recognize in advance whatever agreement might be reached between Japan and Germany as to the disposal of Germany's rights in Shantung; the Japanese Foreign Office also took the opportunity to press for the satisfaction of Japanese claims on several other matters. The 'Twenty-one Demands' were presented in Peking on January 18, 1915. Negotiations went on until May, when, as Yuan proved recalcitrant, compliance with a selected list of the demands was compelled by means of an ultimatum. Two treaties were signed, one granting the transfer to Japan of German rights and privileges in Shantung with an additional railway concession, and the other giving Japan new rights with regard to trade, residence and the leasing of land in South Manchuria and East Inner Mongolia, and an extension of the Kwantung Territory and S.M.R. leases to ninety-nine years.

Submission to the Japanese demands greatly reduced the prestige of Yuan Shih-k'ai and weakened his power. If it had not been for the war in Europe he would not have been at the mercy of Japan as he was in 1915. In that year neither England, France,

nor Russia could afford to oppose, or even rebuke
Japan, and the United States, though distinctly hostile to the Japanese policy, refrained from taking any
decisive steps in the matter. The situation was that
Yuan was isolated, and that, not only diplomatically,
but also financially. His chance of maintaining his
own authority, keeping China united, and improving
her status in international relations depended first
on the diplomatic system of checks and balances
which existed in the Far East after 1905, and, second,
on the flow of foreign credits. Neither of these conditions was fulfilled after the outbreak of the Great
War in 1914, and Yuan was unable either to resist
external pressure from Japan or to hold his power
against domestic revolt. Over-confident because of
his success in 1913, he went on with his project
of making himself Emperor, which led to a rebellion
starting in the south-west and spreading from one
province to another. This time there was no 'reorganization loan' to enable Yuan to prevail; the
European Powers needed all their money to pay for
their own mutual slaughter, Japan was openly hostile, and American bankers were not prepared by
themselves to advance funds. Yuan renounced his
aspiration to the throne and endeavoured to come to
terms with the rebels, but all to no purpose, and in
June 1916 he died from 'eating bitterness'. The republican cause had triumphed, and China entered on
a decade of 'robber baron' anarchy. For the moment
unity seemed to be restored by a compromise be-

tween Yuan's partisans and the Kuomintang, but
civil war burst out afresh within a year, and the military governors in many provinces made themselves
virtually independent of any central control.

As a side-line of her faction struggles China in 1917
declared war on Germany. This 'war' did not, of
course, involve any shooting, but it enabled China
legally to seize German shipping interned in her
ports, expel German traders and missionaries, abrogate German extraterritorial rights, cancel Germany's share in the Boxer indemnity, and claim a
seat at the Peace Conference. Japan had been opposed to China's entry into the war up to the spring
of 1917, but undertook to promote it in her agreement with France, when she received the promise of
French support for the cession of the German Shantung holdings; the step was taken by the Government of Tuan Chi-jui, head of a pro-Japanese military faction which held power in Peking from 1917
to 1920. Japan did not anticipate that China would
make any trouble for her at the Peace Conference, for
Tuan's was the most tractable Chinese Government
with which she had ever had to deal; it was financed
by dubiously secured Japanese loans, which were
promoted by a certain Nishihara acting in a semi-
official capacity on behalf of the Cabinet of Count
Terauchi. But paying attention only to the subservient rulers in Peking, Japan failed to attach due
importance to the growth of an intense nationalist
sentiment among the Chinese intellectuals, who

looked towards Canton for leadership. There a separate Kuomintang Government had come into being, weak as yet in military power, but strong in propaganda appeal both in China and abroad. In order that China might keep up appearances as a single state at the Paris Peace Conference, a delegation had to be formed by compromise between Peking and Canton, and as soon as the Conference opened, it was clear that the delegation was going to represent Chinese nationalist opinion and was quite beyond the reach of Nishihara influence.

Japan, basing her claims on the secret agreements of 1917 with England and France and on the treaty made with China in 1915, as well as on a supplementary agreement of 1918, demanded the cession of the German holdings in Shantung. China asked for their immediate restoration to herself, maintaining that her entry into the war 'had completely altered her status', and had abrogated Germany's treaty rights so that there was no longer anything for the Germans to cede. China also challenged the validity of the 1915 treaty, alleging that it had been signed under duress. The Japanese delegate pointed out that at any rate the treaty of 1918 had not been signed after an ultimatum, and that the Germans had been evicted from Kiaochow, not by a Chinese declaration, but by a campaign of the Japanese army. The controversy became extremely embittered and the other leading Powers were dragged in, only, however, to aggravate the dissension. England and France adhered to the 1917 treaties and upheld the Japanese claim; the American delegation, on the other hand, took up a strongly pro-Chinese attitude. President Wilson refused to be bound by the pledges given to Japan by England and France. Negotiations came to a deadlock, and the Japanese delegates, following the example of the Italians, who had left Paris because of Wilson's opposition to their claims (likewise based on inter-Allied secret treaties), threatened to withdraw unless their demands were met. In the end Wilson consented to the cession of the German holdings to Japan, and the Japanese delegation gave a verbal assurance that it was their country's intention to hand back the leased territory to China at a date not specified. Germany made the cession in three articles of the Treaty of Versailles, which China accordingly refused to sign.

Wilson had given way because of his intense desire to include all the major Allied Powers in the League of Nations and his fear that it would be ineffective for Far Eastern problems if Japan were outside it. But the surrender was extremely distasteful to him. 'Of all the important decisions at the Conference,' writes Mr. Stannard Baker, 'none worried him so much and none finally satisfied him less.' Well might it have worried him, for no section of the Treaty of Versailles was to be used against him with more telling effect in the anti-Wilson campaign of the Republicans which resulted in America's non-ratification of the Versailles Treaty and abstention from membership of the League of Nations! A volume of pro-Chinese and anti-Japanese sentiment which had been accumulating in America for several years suddenly burst forth with extraordinary violence. Wilson had abandoned the cause of China in order to gain Japan's signature to the Covenant of the League, but he found on his return to America that he had put a deadly weapon into the hands of the Covenant's enemies in his own country. The Covenant itself was a target for criticism, but the heaviest fire was directed at the Treaty settlement with which it was bound up, and no part of it was so shocking to American opinion as the Shantung cession. Ever since 1911 there had prevailed in the U.S.A. a romantic cult of the 'sister republic' of China, fostered by enthusiastic American missionaries who believed it to be a field ripe for the Christian harvest, and skilfully worked up by propaganda of American-educated Chinese nationalists. This sympathetic, protective attitude towards China was not, indeed, free from an element of condescension; as an American writer puts it : 'We seldom, as a nation, feel much affection for people we cannot be sorry for.' Formerly, Americans had had just this kind of patronizing enthusiasm for Japan, as for a child clever beyond its years and oppressed by European bullies; but feeling had undergone a great change since Japan had begun to assume the style and diplomatic habits of a Great Power and to exclude American capital from Manchuria. Exasperation against Japan had grown *pari passu* with the increase of sympathy for China as for a nation struggling to be, not only independent, but also democratic. The sentiment thus engendered was a powerful factor in turning the American public against Wilson and his Treaty, and it expressed itself also in discriminatory legislation against Japanese immigrants in California and other Western States.

Japan thus achieved her purpose with regard to Shantung at the Paris Peace Conference, but only at the cost of arousing a dangerous antagonism both in China and in the United States. Her two other gains at the Peace Conference were a League of Nations mandate for the German island groups of the Pacific north of the Equator and admission to a permanent seat on the Council of the League—a distinction which formally ranked her as a Great Power. But these results also were subject to qualifications which robbed them of much of their value. The Japanese failed either to obtain the German islands in full sovereignty or to get inserted in the Covenant of the League a declaration of the principle of racial equality. The application of the mandate system to the former German islands meant that they could not be fortified, and their potential strategic value was so far lost to Japan. The mandate restrictions could not, however, be regarded as a matter for grievance as long as they were applied equally to all the German colonies which had fallen into the hands of the Allies. It was otherwise with the rebuff to Japan over her racial equality proposal; it was differential treatment of her nationals which Japan sought to abolish by getting the race equality principle incorporated in the League Covenant, and her failure to achieve this object only emphasized the colour-line drawn by the United States and the British Dominions. The Japanese delegation proposed that the parties to the Covenant should agree 'to accord, as soon as possible, to all alien nationals of states members of the League equal and just treatment in every respect, making no distinction, either in law or in fact, on account of their race or nationality'. The proposal in a modified form was eventually put to the Drafting Commission and obtained eleven out of seventeen votes, but was ruled out by President Wilson as Chairman on the ground that unanimity was required for such a resolution. As a Japanese writer remarks:[1] 'This bitter experience, with which the name of Woodrow Wilson is indelibly associated, . . . left the profoundest impression upon the Japanese mind.'

[1] R. H. Akagi, *Japan's Foreign Relations 1542–1936*, p. 325.

X

THE WASHINGTON TREATIES

THE Peace Treaties of 1919 left the Far East under the domination of three Great Powers—England, the United States, and Japan. Of the three other nations which had ranked as regional Great Powers in the pre-war period, Germany was definitely eliminated, having lost not only her stronghold at Tsingtao, but also all her extraterritorial and settlement rights in China. France retained her possessions, but had greatly declined in relative importance since 1898 owing to preoccupation with European affairs, and was now more than ever concentrated in Europe. Russia, turned Communist and at odds with all capitalist nations, was for the time being paralysed by civil war.

Of the three Great Powers remaining in 1919, Japan was on very bad terms with the United States, a development which placed England in a difficult position. When the Anglo-Japanese alliance was originally formed, it did not occur to the British Foreign Office that it might one day become incompatible with Anglo-American friendship. Friction between Japan and the U.S.A. only began after the Russo-Japanese war, but by the end of 1910, after the frustration of the Knox neutralization scheme, Japanese-American relations were so strained that British opinion began to fear an alienation from the United States as a consequence of the alliance with Japan. There was even a demand in some quarters for a decision not to renew the alliance when its term expired—a step which might have been disastrous for England, for a German-Japanese alliance would probably have been the sequel. To meet the new objections to the Japanese connexion without losing this essential element in the anti-German coalition, the British Government proposed a revision of the alliance treaty, absolving the parties from the obligation to go to war against a third Power with whom either of them might have a treaty of general arbitration. This provision was meant to exclude the possibility of England being compelled by the terms of the alliance to side with Japan in a war against the United States, for England was at the time negotiating an arbitration treaty with the U.S.A. and expected it to come into force shortly. As it turned out, however, the American Senate did not ratify the arbitration treaty, and so the clause in the new Anglo-Japanese alliance treaty did not have the intended effect. Nevertheless, it was made clear to Japan that England did not intend the alliance ever to have an anti-American point and would certainly not fight for Japan in a Japanese-American quarrel.

After the decision of the war of 1914–18 Japanese-American antagonism was accentuated, and there was no longer any adequate political ground for the Anglo-Japanese alliance even in the limited liability

form it assumed in 1911. In its original form it had
stood for a common interest of the two Powers. Both
England and Japan had been desperately anxious to
prevent a Russian hegemony in the Far East. After
the Russo-Japanese war England had more need of
the alliance than Japan, for Japan was not inevitably
Germany's foe, and she had been held in the orbit
of the anti-German coalition by a *tolerari potest* for
her annexation of Korea and assertion of an exclusive sphere in South Manchuria. But with the collapse of Germany in 1918 the situation was entirely
altered. The German menace was removed, as the
Russian menace had been thirteen years earlier, and
there was no longer any common enemy to hold
England and Japan together. The alliance had
had first an anti-Russian point and then an anti-
German point. Both the trials by war having been
decided, Japan's conflict with America took the centre
of the stage, and here England and Japan parted
company. After the signing of the Peace Treaties
the alliance was regarded as not merely superfluous,
but also dangerous for England, and British statesmen studied how they could decently get rid of it.

The bloc England-France-Japan-Russia was now
dissolved. Its two main factors of cohesion in the
region of the Far East had been the Anglo-Japanese
alliance and the Russo-Japanese monopoly-sharing
partnership in Manchuria. Both of these combina-
tions were now broken up. The Russo-Japanese
entente had indeed been wiped out entirely, for the

old Tsarist Russia had ceased to be, whereas there was still a residue of sympathy and will to co-operation between Japan and England. As the strength of Japan's position *vis-à-vis* America had previously depended largely on the diplomatic support of England and Russia (manifested so clearly in 1910), the loss of that support was a very serious matter for Japanese foreign policy. Japan found herself diplomatically isolated. Of the four states with which she was in closest contact, China and the United States were definitely hostile, England was frigidly neutral, and Russia—the new Russia of the Soviets—was an enemy in arms. It was true that both England and the U.S.A. had a common interest with Japan in opposing the spread of Bolshevism, and were actually co-operating with her in an interventionist expedition to Siberia. But the common cause of anti-Bolshevism was insufficient to secure harmony between the policies of the three Powers, and such co-operation as there was came to an end with the withdrawal of the American contingent from Siberia in January 1920.

The Allied intervention in Siberia had begun as a sequel to the outbreak of fighting between the Soviets and the Czecho-Slovak legionaries in May 1918. When the Bolshevik Government stopped Russia's war against Germany and entered into negotiations for a separate peace, the small army recruited from Czech prisoners and deserters, which had been fighting in the Russian line against the

Austrians, declared its intention of going to the Western front to assist further in the struggle on which Czech national freedom depended. Owing to the difficulties and dangers of the route by Archangel it was decided to transport the Czech troops by the Trans-Siberian railway to Vladivostok and there embark them to be taken to Europe by the Panama Canal. Trouble arose on various issues between the Czech detachments—some of whose officers were Russians of White sympathies—and local Soviet authorities, and the situation was complicated by the presence in Siberia of large numbers of liberated German and Austrian prisoners of war who were hostile to the Czechs and were also trying to get hold of rolling stock. After a fight between Czechs and Red Guards at Cheliabinsk War Commissar Trotsky issued a peremptory order to local Soviets to disarm the Czechs and commanded that 'every Czech who is found armed on the railway is to be shot on the spot'. The Czechs replied to this imprudent forcefulness by seizing all the principal stations from Samara on the Volga to Vladivostok and assuming control of the whole Trans-Siberian line; theirs was the only large body of disciplined troops left in Russia at this time, and it was more than a match for any Soviet forces which could be brought against it. There is no evidence, however, that the Czech leaders had originally any intention of fighting the Soviets or intervening in Russian domestic disputes; their one idea was to get out of

Russia and make their way to the Western front as quickly as possible.[1] If Trotsky had had more tact and less blind faith in the virtue of 'shooting on the spot', he could easily have got rid of the Czechs and avoided any clash more serious than a petty local brawl. But once open warfare had begun, the scattered detachments of Czechs could only hold their own by suppressing the Soviets which were trying to disarm them, and this gave a longed-for opportunity both to the anti-Bolshevik Russians within the areas involved and to the political elements in the Allied countries which favoured an anti-Bolshevik intervention. The Czech victories made it possible for Russian counter-revolutionary governments to be set up in places where the Soviets had been overthrown, and on August 3, 1918, Allied intervention began at the Far Eastern end with the landing of Japanese and British troops at Vladivostok, soon to be followed by an American contingent from the Philippines and a French one from Indo-China.

In this invasion of Russian territory the aims common to the Allied Governments were the relief of the Czechs, the recovery of munition stocks sent to Russia via Siberia for use against Germany, and support for the Russian counter-revolution. In Japan, however, there was a political group which hoped in addition to use the intervention for pur-

[1] See W. H. Chamberlin, *The Russian Revolution 1917–1921*, vol. ii, pp. 2–8, for a summary of the course of events.

poses of territorial aggrandizement. This group was never in full control of Japanese policy, but it was strong enough to make the intervention into a large-scale military enterprise which might be expected to yield results of the kind desired by the mere impetus of its operations. The opposition to schemes of Siberian conquest came from various sections of opinion, and not only from liberals. Among those who rejected a 'positive' expansionist policy for Japan were many who believed that the acquisition of Siberian territory would bar the way to a *rapprochement* with Russia, whatever type of Government might finally emerge there, would not yield economic results commensurate with the costs of occupation and defence, and would dissipate strength which was more urgently needed for the backing of Japanese diplomacy *vis-à-vis* China and the U.S.A. Naval circles in particular deprecated a programme of continental expansion which would leave Japan with an enormous land frontier and necessitate a heavy increase of military expenditure just at the time when competition in naval armaments was imposing a heavy financial strain on the country.

Detachments of the Allied forces occupied the chief towns of Siberia east of Lake Baikal in the autumn of 1918 and remained in them all through 1919, while the Government set up at Omsk under Admiral Kolchak was making its effort to overthrow the Soviet régime west of the Urals. There was, however, no co-ordination of policies among the

cc

intervening Powers, and the actions of the various contingents reflected the divergence of national aims. The British and French supported Admiral Kolchak; the Japanese, hoping to detach East Siberia from the rest of Russia, supported the locally independent Cossack atamans Semyenov and Kalmikov; the American commander, General Graves, was hostile to Kolchak, Semyenov, and Kalmikov alike, and openly sympathetic to left-wing elements. Relations between the American and Japanese commands were extremely strained. The joint intervention came to an end at the beginning of 1920 after the collapse of the Whites and the advance of the Reds from the Urals to Lake Baikal. The British, French, and Americans now withdrew, and the Japanese were left to carry on by themselves. After the departure of the American troops the Washington Government showed itself distinctly antagonistic to the continued Japanese occupation; the desire to crush Bolshevism had by this time been superseded by an anxiety to keep the door open for economic advantages which might be expected from a reconciliation with the Soviet régime. The Americans had no intention of allowing Japan to take Russia's Pacific ports and enclose a possible field for their trade and enterprise. Their attitude found expression in a note addressed to Japan on May 31, 1921, in which it was roundly declared that 'the Government of the United States can neither now nor hereafter recognize as valid any claims or titles arising out of the present occupation and control, and it cannot acquiesce in any action taken by the Government of Japan which might impair existing treaty rights or the political or territorial integrity of Russia'.

America's opposition, added to the inherent difficulties of holding territory in Siberia without any cause sufficient to rally Japanese political opinion solidly behind the promoters, led in the end to the liquidation of the Siberian adventure. Had it not been for the massacre of Japanese residents and a detachment of troops at Nikolaievsk in March 1920 the evacuation would probably have been completed in that year, but feeling was so much stirred by the episode that there was a temporary revival of military activity. Transbaikalia was finally abandoned in the autumn, but Vladivostok was not evacuated until October 1922, and the Russian half of Sakhalin was retained until after the conclusion of the Soviet-Japanese treaty of 1925. No *quid pro quo* was obtained for the withdrawal from the mainland, but long-term concession rights for the exploitation of coal- and oil-fields were secured for Japanese companies in northern Sakhalin before it was restored to Russian rule.

The costly commitment of the Siberian expedition, for which 70,000 men had been sent out, was not the only embarrassment of the Japanese Government in the years 1919–21. Japan was simultaneously being harried by a Chinese nationalist boycott and hard pressed by the strain of a naval armaments race with the United States. Her situation was both politically and economically very unfavourable, for she was isolated diplomatically as she had never been since 1901, and was at the same time financially distressed. The war-time trade boom, which had brought temporary prosperity, had led to a mushroom growth of unsound enterprises and a corresponding spate of bankruptcies in the post-war period, so that the country was in a poor condition for sustaining a truculent foreign policy. Business circles desired the restoration of normal trade with China and the strengthening of national credit by an improvement of relations with Washington and London ; they were also anxious to lighten the heavy burden of taxation by retrenchment in military and naval expenditure. These requirements of commerce and industry converged with a rapid growth of liberal political forces due to the apparent verdict of the Great War in favour of democracy and internationalism. The overthrow of the three great semiautocratic monarchies of Germany, Austria, and Russia, and the failure in war of that 'Prussian militarism', which the leaders of the Japanese army had taken as their model, greatly reduced the prestige of the military-bureaucratic system of government within Japan. A new radicalism appeared in Japanese politics, and the older generation of 'clan' statesmen found themselves confronted with a strong popular demand for universal suffrage, responsibility of the Cabinet to the Diet, a widening of civil rights and various measures of social reform. This liberal tendency was to provide the key-note of Japanese political development in the decade 1920–30. There was not in the first half of the decade any serious Communist agitation. The menace of proletarian revolution only began to disturb the minds of Japan's rulers after 1925 and not to any great extent until 1930. From 1920 to 1925 the progressive movement bore an almost exclusively bourgeois-democratic character. Its political party was the Kenseikai, which on reorganization later took the name of Minseito. This party specially represented the main interests of heavy industry and the textile manufacturers, and was opposed by the more conservative Seiyukai, associated with agrarian interests and the chauvinist military group. The division between the two big parties of the Diet corresponded to some extent to the cleavage on matters of policy between the two fighting services. The Navy, lacking the Army's close connexion with the interests of the landowners, and opposed to its schemes of Continental expansion, inclined towards the cause of the Minseito in domestic politics, and the Minseito politicians, averse to expensive territorial aggrandizement, but believing in a strong navy for national security and protection of maritime trade, were more ready to favour the Navy than the Army in budget expenditures and policy consultations. The semi-independent status given to the fighting services

by Japanese constitutional practice in the period between the Sino-Japanese and Russo-Japanese wars
meant that the Army and Navy were active political
forces with which civilian statesmen had to deal.
No cabinet could be formed unless a general and an
admiral on the active list could be found to serve in
it, and in case of a measure which was thoroughly
unpopular with one or other of the fighting services
its representative in the Cabinet could wreck the
ministry by resigning. The power of the services,
however, depended largely on their ability to combine in putting pressure on the civilians, and the
differences of opinion between the Army and Navy
were of great importance in enabling the liberals to
make headway against the military-conservative
ascendancy.

In foreign policy the liberals called for all-round
conciliation and a settlement of Japan's three great
conflicts—with the new Soviet Russia, with China,
and with the United States. Their agitation was
effective, and their success was reflected in the
gradual liquidation of the Siberian adventure, in the
restoration of Kiaochow to China in 1922, and in
the treaties concluded at the Washington Conference
in the same year.

In China the Treaty of Versailles, with its cession
of the German Shantung leasehold to Japan, had
created intense indignation among the politically
minded, and a boycott campaign had been directed
against Japan. The weapon of boycott, made effec-

tive by intimidation of traders who did not willingly
participate, had already been used against Japan by
Chinese patriots on three occasions, but it had never
been so damaging to Japanese commerce as it was
in 1919. For the first time Chinese nationalism
appeared as a force which had to be taken seriously,
and its new strength in action was all the more remarkable because it was contemporary with a
greater degree of disintegration of the state than
China had known since the T'ai P'ing rebellion.
The new nationalist spirit had its strongholds outside the strictly political sphere, and was therefore
able to exert nation-wide influence in spite of the
division of the country between warring factions.
Its centres of power were the schools and univer-
sities which had been founded everywhere to provide Western-type education and had usurped the
prestige of learning, formerly the possession of the
Confucian *literati*.

The severity of the boycott induced the Japanese
exporting industries, largely dependent on the
Chinese market, to put pressure on their Government for a settlement with China. Japan had undertaken verbally at the Paris Peace Conference to
restore the German properties to China, but it was
generally expected that Japan would drive a hard
bargain over the conditions of the transfer and retain in Shantung a degree of control which would
assimilate that province to South Manchuria. The
Japanese legal position was a strong one, for the

cession to Japan without any promise of restoration was written in the Treaty of Versailles, and none of the ex-Allied signatories could question the clauses dealing with Shantung without making a breach in the sacrosanct Versailles system. There could be no diplomatic support for revision from England or France, and Washington was not likely to make a direct attack on the Paris settlement in spite of American public sympathy for China's case. Nevertheless, Japan adopted a very conciliatory attitude and gradually the tension relaxed. China at first refused to negotiate at all on the basis of the Versailles Treaty, which she had refused to sign, but in the end she consented to discuss terms of transfer, and a settlement of the question was reached on February 4, 1922, as a by-product of the Washington Conference. Certain purely economic concessions were granted to Japan, but the Kiaochow territory and the Tsingtao-Tsinan railway were fully restored to China, and the preferential rights were renounced, so that Japan retained no instrument for building up in Shantung a semi-colonial system such as existed in Manchuria. This agreement certainly improved Sino-Japanese relations, and appeared to open up a prospect of a real *détente* between the two states. Unfortunately the conflict of their policies was too fundamental for the improvement to be maintained.

Japan's third trouble—the dangerous naval rivalry with the United States—was settled for fourteen years by the Washington Naval Treaty signed on February 6, 1922. The naval rivalry was sharpened by the conflicts of general policy between the two countries, but, like the Anglo-German naval rivalry before 1914, it became in itself a more serious cause of alarm and enmity than any clash of interests. The situation which confronted Japan after the close of the Great War was the result of America's great war effort, which had led to an immense increase of her fighting power, a new consciousness of strength, and—in some quarters—a new conception of the manner in which American foreign policy should be conducted. There appeared to be a golden future for American trade and investment in the Far East if Japan could be prevented from enclosing a great part of the market, for this was judged to be the aim behind the Japanese military occupations in Shantung and Siberia. The way to frustrate Japan and keep her bottled up within her own borders was to have an American naval superiority not only in the Eastern, but also in the Western, Pacific, and for this purpose it was necessary both to increase the existing lead in tonnage of warships and to construct adequate bases in the Philippines and at Guam. Japan was greatly alarmed at the prospect of American competition, for there was no doubt of America's financial capacity to outbuild Japan in a naval armaments race, if she had the will, or of her right to construct bases in her own sovereign possessions. Japanese naval power, on the other hand,

DD

would be hampered by the fact that the former German islands in the Pacific—which lay across the routes from Hawaii to the Philippines—had been granted to her, not in full sovereignty, but only under a League of Nations mandate which did not permit them to be fortified. If America were to carry through resolutely a programme of building up a naval hegemony in the Pacific, Japan would have to resign herself to a progressive alteration of the ratios of power in the Far East in favour of her rival— unless she were to strike at an early stage of the process while she still had an advantage in the matter of bases. There is perhaps no factor which drives a state into war so inexorably as a steady loss of relative power. Sooner or later a desperate now-or-never mood overcomes the calculations of prudence, and the belief that a war may be won to-day, but cannot be won to-morrow, becomes the most convincing of all arguments for an appeal to the sword. It was so with Austria in 1914, and Japan was not far from the critical point when naval construction beyond the limits of the budget was financed by propaganda-promoted public subscription.

But the climax of the process was not reached because on neither side was there a sufficiency of will to enter on a decisive struggle. In both countries there was a general desire for a return to what President Harding called 'normalcy', and American opinion was somewhat reassured by signs of a weakening of chauvinist pressure behind Japan's foreign policy. In these circumstances the American Government, after preliminary soundings, issued formal invitations on August 11, 1921, to the Four Principal Allied Powers (England, France, Italy, and Japan) 'to participate in a conference on the limitation of armaments, in connexion with which Pacific and Far Eastern questions would also be discussed'. The success achieved by the Washington Conference was due primarily to the scope of the initial proposal, for no attempt was made to separate the issue of arms limitation from general political problems. As the American delegation stated in a report of the Conference to the President:

'The declared object was, in its naval aspect, to stop the race of competitive building of warships which was in progress and which was so distressingly like the competition that immediately preceded the war of 1914. Competitive armament, however, is the result of a state of mind in which a national expectation of attack by some other country causes preparation to meet the attack. To stop competition it is necessary to deal with the state of mind from which it results. A belief in the pacific intentions of other Powers must be substituted for suspicion and apprehension.'

The two most important agreements resulting from the Washington Conference were the Nine-Power Treaty of February 6, 1922, 'relating to principles and policies to be followed in matters concerning China' and the Five-Power Limitation of Naval Armaments Treaty of the same date. The first of these instruments was meant to terminate once and for all the scramble for concessions and spheres in China and at the same time to placate Chinese nationalism. The signatories of the Treaty (the British Empire, the U.S.A., Japan, France, Italy, Holland, Belgium, Portugal, and China herself) agreed:

1. To respect the sovereignty, the independence, and the territorial and administrative integrity of China;

2. To provide the fullest and most unembarrassed opportunity to China to develop and maintain for herself an effective and stable Government;

3. To use their influence for the purpose of effectually establishing and maintaining the principle of equal opportunity for the commerce and industry of all nations throughout the territory of China;

4. To refrain from taking advantage of conditions in China in order to seek special rights or privileges which would abridge the rights of subjects or citizens of friendly States, and from countenancing action inimical to the security of such States.

The terms of this treaty, coupled with a Japanese undertaking to complete the evacuation of Siberia, provided the essential political conditions for the Naval Treaty signed by England, the United States, Japan, France, and Italy. The Naval Treaty provided for the 5 : 5 : 3 ratio for tonnage of capital ships as between England, the U.S.A. and Japan, and for the maintenance of the *status quo* as regards forti-

fications and naval bases in a specified area of the
Pacific. The Japanese at first held out for a 10 : 10 : 7
ratio, but agreed to the 5 : 5 : 3 on condition that
the *status quo* for fortifications was accepted. All
things considered, they made a very good bargain.
The ratio of capital ships was ultimately less important to them than a guarantee against the construction of first-class naval bases at Hong Kong or Manila.
The standstill agreement covered Hong Kong, the
Philippines, Guam, Formosa, the Ryukyu, Bonin,
Kurile, and Aleutian Islands. Japan thus contributed
parts of her island chain to the common pool, but
was secured against new British or American naval
base development nearer to her shores than Hawaii
or Singapore. The result was

'to make the defensive position of Japan in the Western
Pacific absolutely impregnable by sea, and thus not only
to safeguard Japan herself against any attack or invasion
but to assure one of the chief objects of her policy—the
object for which she had been building up her great
navy—which was the uninterrupted security of her communications in wartime with her continental possessions
and with China'.[1]

A third Washington agreement to which consider-
able importance was attached at the time was the
Four-Power Treaty of December 13, 1921, relating
to 'Insular Possessions and Insular Dominions in the
Pacific Ocean'. The four Powers were the British
Empire, the U.S.A., Japan, and France. They

[1] Arnold J. Toynbee, *Survey of International Affairs, 1920–3*, p. 490.

mutually agreed to respect the *status quo* with regard to Pacific islands (from which category Japan Proper was excluded), and to confer together on any dispute arising between any two of them or in the event of a threat from an outside Power. This treaty did not touch on any matter of real conflict and contained no alliance obligations. Nor has it ever been an important diplomatic instrument. But it was never really meant to be the foundation of a new grouping of Powers; its real function was to provide a decent interment for the Anglo-Japanese alliance, which was to terminate on the ratification of the new Four-Power pact by its signatories. England's partnership with Japan, which had stood the test of two wars but had been practically inoperative since 1918, was thus brought to an end, and no two of the Powers in the Far East were any longer bound together by alliance commitments apart from the general 'sanctions' obligations under the Covenant of the League of Nations.

The Washington Conference certainly produced a *détente* between Japan and the United States, and seemed to promise a new era of peace and stability in the Far East. The promise was not fulfilled, for the lull that followed the Conference was destined to be of very short duration. But the new storm that broke in 1925 belongs to another chapter of history; it was not merely a recrudescence of the troubles which had vexed diplomacy in the period from 1895 to 1922. The main problems for solution had been set hitherto by the encroachments of foreign Powers on the sove-reignty and integrity of China and by the jealousies and rivalries arising out of the encroachments. Except for the futile and retrograde Boxer outbreak, China had been the helpless and passive subject of the activities of other nations, to be coerced or protected against coercion, to be advised or reproved, but never herself a major factor of original movement and volition. With the administrative collapse and confusion of the civil wars which had been going on since 1917, China seemed to be less than ever capable of looking after herself or taking a strong initiative of any kind. The problem, as seen by the diplomats at the Washington Conference, was how to preserve China against further encroachments, how to get pledges from all concerned for a general 'Hands off China' policy. It was supposed that if, in the words of the Nine-Power Treaty, the foreign Powers were to give China 'the fullest and most un-embarrassed opportunity' to set her house in order and were to 'refrain from taking advantage of conditions in order to seek special rights or privileges', then China would fall in with the plan by devoting herself to domestic reform and reconstruction, so that there would be an end of trouble, for some time at any rate, both between China and the foreign Powers and between the various foreign Powers about China. What was not anticipated at the Washington Conference was that China, now sheltered from aggression as she had never been before, would herself

'take advantage of conditions' to launch, with every
means at her disposal short of regular warfare, a
furious revisionist campaign against already existing
treaty rights. But this was exactly what happened.
It was not enough that the privileged Powers should
cease to advance; Chinese nationalism demanded
that they should retreat. The foreign Powers might
delude themselves with the belief that they had only
to renounce further conquests for the peace and
tranquillity of the Far East to be assured. But it was
now China's turn to attack. There was to be no
'close of play' in 1922, no security for the *status quo*.
It has been said that the weakest moment for a des-
potism is when it begins to reform; the weakest moment likewise for the Powers which had imposed
servitudes on Chinese sovereignty was when they
agreed together to 'provide the fullest and most un-
embarrassed opportunity to China'—to carry through
a nationalist revolution.

XI

THE MARCH OF THE KUOMINTANG

AT the time of the Washington Conference in 1921–2 there were in China, besides a number of quasi-independent military governors of provinces, two organized Governments, one at Peking and one at Canton. Of these rival authorities the former was the one which was recognized as legitimate by other nations, Peking having been the capital of China for five centuries and the foreign Legations having been established there. The rulers at Canton were, therefore, technically rebels, and the foreign Powers took up a juridically correct attitude in insisting that the surplus of the foreign-administered Maritime Customs (after all charges for loans and indemnities secured on this revenue had been met) should be handed over to the Government in Peking. The Customs administration was thus bound to remit payment to Peking from Canton itself, and when in 1923 Sun Yat-sen, in desperate straits for money, threatened to seize the Customs House he was dissuaded from his purpose by a naval demonstration in which British, French, American, Japanese, Portuguese, and Italian units took part.

It was nevertheless from Canton, and not from Peking, that China's new political unity was destined to emerge. For Canton was the head-quarters of the Revolution, and the Revolution, whatever form it

might take, was the only living force in China.
There could not be any future in China for mere
conservatism, for an inert resistance to change and
prolongation of the nineteenth-century past—so recent in time and yet so utterly remote and incom-
prehensible for the Western-educated Chinese of the
younger generation. The old order had passed for
ever with the substitution of a Western-patterned
educational curriculum for the old Confucian classical schooling from 1901 onwards, and the abolition
of the monarchy in 1912 had been a natural sequel
to the abrupt ideological break with the past. But
although the *ancien régime* was in ruins, there did not
exist between 1912 and 1926 any organized political
force capable of replacing it and creating a new
order to meet the demands of a revolutionary situation. Hence, over the greater part of China power
fell into the hands of men who were survivors of
the old order, who accepted the Republic but were
not of it, who had seen the irremediable collapse
of the old world of Chinese tradition, but had no
understanding of the new world of ideas and institutions imported into China from the West. Such
men were Wu P'ei-fu, who had taken the degree
of *hsiu-ts'ai* under the old classical examination
system in 1894, and Chang Tso-lin, who had started
his career as a brigand in Manchuria. These two
represented respectively the more and the less culti-
vated types to be found among the soldiers and
officials holding power in Peking in the interval

between the abdication of the Manchu dynasty and the march of the Kuomintang from Canton to the Amur.

Lacking a political cause or a coherent ideology as a basis of principle since the break-down of the old Confucian orthodoxy, without either a popular party organization to sustain them from below or a legitimate monarchy to endow them with its sovereign right, the coteries of generals and bureaucrats who strove for control of the Peking Government were quite incapable of giving China a stable and efficient administration or of formulating a constructive policy. Their power depended on private armies financed by the revenues of provinces, which were intercepted by military governors so that they never reached the Peking treasury. The Peking Government was not, therefore, a real authority with its own budget—the revenue directly remitted to it was virtually limited to the Maritime Customs surplus—but was the puppet of the strongest faction of the provincial despots, and its composition and policy were decided by wars fought between the most powerful military chiefs with the mastery of the capital as the objective.

The details of the civil wars would have no significance for these pages were it not for their effect on the status of Manchuria—an international issue of the greatest importance. The Northern generals were divided into three factions named after the provinces with which they were particularly associated—the Anfu (Anhui) led by Tuan Chi-jui, the Chihli led by Ts'ao K'un and Wu P'ei-fu, and the Fengtien (province of Manchuria, now Liaoning) led by Chang Tso-lin. The Anfu faction was predominant in Peking from 1917 to 1920; then it was overthrown by a combination of the Chihli and Fengtien forces. But in 1922 the victors quarrelled, and Chang Tso-lin was forced to retire north of the Great Wall. A Peking Government subservient to the Chihli generals stripped him of his official rank, but he ignored the sentence delivered from the capital and, secluded from China Proper by barriers of sea and mountain, made himself *de facto* the absolute monarch of Manchuria. He had been virtually an independent ruler ever since he had been appointed Inspector-General of the Three Eastern Provinces in 1918; now he was in open rebellion against Peking, and his *de facto* independence meant that he was in a position to prevent the fulfilment of any international treaty concluded by the Peking Foreign Office. A difficulty of this kind arose when in 1924 the Peking Government concluded a treaty with the Soviet Union making the latter the heir to the rights of the vanished Tsarist Russia in the Chinese Eastern Railway and laying down regulations for the management of the line. This agreement was a remarkable one in view of all that had happened, for not only had the Soviet Government in 1919 announced its intention of making a free restoration to China both of the railway and of all privileges connected with it, but the Chinese Government had in 1920 made an agreement about the working of the line with the Russo-Asiatic Bank (heir of Witte's Russo-Chinese Bank) which now had its head-quarters in Paris and claimed to be the sole shareholder of the Railway Company. Yet both the Soviet declaration of policy and the Chinese agreement with the Bank were scrapped when negotiations for a Sino-Soviet Treaty, involving the recognition of the Soviet Union by China, were started in Peking. The Soviet diplomats demanded the transfer to their state of the Russian rights in the railway which Tsarist imperialism had constructed with French capital and Chinese labour, and in spite of protests from the French and American Ministers the Peking Government gave its consent.

Three motives are discernible in this act of policy: first, to obtain a treaty on 'equal' terms (for, as the Soviet had made the gesture of renouncing the Tsarist rights, their re-cession could be represented as a free grant); second, to bring Russia in again as a check on Japanese penetration in Manchuria; and third, to embarrass Chang Tso-lin, who, as satrap of Manchuria, was the near neighbour of the Soviet power and very ill-disposed towards it. The third motive was probably the strongest of the three, and its presence was recognized by Chang Tso-lin who declined to be bound by the agreement. He was nevertheless in an awkward position. He could not afford to provoke a Russian attack on his rear

while he needed all his strength to keep the Chihli
army out of Manchuria, and he was also aware that
he could not expect the 'Treaty Powers', even though
their sympathies might be anti-Soviet, to support
him in the cancellation of a treaty properly concluded by the recognized Government of China.
Chang therefore took refuge in a compromise. He
agreed to admit the Soviet Union to the rights ceded
by the Peking-Soviet Treaty, but he insisted on the
signature of a separate treaty with himself, differing
in details from the document signed in Peking. Thus
he repudiated the right of the Peking Government
to make a treaty with a foreign Power on a specifi-
cally Manchurian question without his consent, and
the Soviet Government endorsed his pretension by
negotiating a new treaty directly with Chang Tso-lin
(styled 'Agreement between the Autonomous Government of the Three Eastern Provinces of the Republic
of China and the Government of the Union of Soviet
Socialist Republics'). As a distinguished writer on
international affairs has pointed out,[1]

'the one significant fact about the Mukden agreement
was that it recognized Marshal Chang's Government of
the Three Eastern Provinces (i.e. Fengtien, Heilungkiang
and Kirin, which together make up Manchuria) practically on the footing of a separate and independent state,
and this at a time when he was in open rebellion against
the Central Government.'

Peking was naturally indignant, but the Soviet

[1] A. Toynbee, *Survey of International Affairs, 1925*, vol. ii, p. 336.

Government was impatient to get the railway into
its hands, and it was soon saved from the nuisance
of Peking protests by the break-up of the Chihli
faction and the triumph of a new combination
including Chang Tso-lin, who thereby ceased to be
a 'rebel'. The Mukden-Soviet Treaty, nevertheless,
created a precedent dangerous for China, and Chang
Tso-lin's assumption of sovereignty in 1924 paved
the way for the proclamation of the independence
of Manchukuo in 1932.

While these events were taking place in relation
to the Government at Peking, a very different political development was going on at Canton. The
Canton Government was not simply the instrument
of a military clique, but was an emanation of the
Kuomintang or Nationalist Party, an elaborately
organized political body with a strong basis of
popular support and a definite programme. The
Kuomintang dated from 1912; it replaced an older
association, Sun Yat-sen's T'ungmenghui, which was
founded in 1907 and was the principal promoter of
the demand for a Republic in 1911. The T'ungmenghui and its successor represented the revolutionary idea of Canton, an idea compounded of the
traditional anti-Manchu and anti-Peking sentiment
of the south and the progressive ardour of the
southern coastal cities, which had been longest and
most intimately in contact with Western civilization,
not only through maritime trade but also through
their emigrant communities in California, Hawaii,

Malaya, and Java. The Cantonese radicals had hoped
to lead China after the Revolution of 1911, but they
were frustrated by the conservatism and anti-Can-
tonese sentiment of the north. The Kuomintang
was proscribed by Yuan Shih-k'ai in 1913 and again
by the Anfu Cabinet in power at Peking in 1917.
Thereafter the Revolution retreated to its base and
a separate Kuomintang Government, claiming to be
the *de jure* authority of the Republic, was set up at
Canton. In 1921 Sun Yat-sen was elected 'President of the Chinese Republic' by Kuomintang members of the disbanded national Parliament.

The effective rule of the Canton Government did
not extend far beyond the limits of the city. For its
military power it was until 1925 dependent on mercenaries, and this fact involved it in internal dissensions disastrous to its cause, for the rapacity of
the garrison troops recruited mainly from the inland
provinces of Kwangsi and Yunnan made them
very unpopular with the citizens of Canton. A revolt
in 1922, led by General Ch'en Ch'iung-ming, forced
Sun Yat-sen to flee from Canton, but he returned
the following year and laid an even heavier burden of
condottiere exactions on his capital city. The mercenaries were much happier plundering the wealthy
port of Canton than taking the field against the
northern armies, and as long as Sun was alive he
was too busy holding Canton in subjection to undertake any serious campaign outside Kwangtung province.

The power of the Kuomintang, however, was not to be measured by the extent of the sway of the Canton Government. The party was nation-wide and even in the provinces ruled by Chihli and Fengtien 'war-lords' it represented Chinese public opinion. Just as the Catholic Church extended far and wide beyond the temporal domination of the Papal States, so the Kuomintang permeated the whole of China even while its Government could scarcely maintain itself in one province. The principal medium of its spread was the student class, which was everywhere imbued with revolutionary enthusiasm, iconoclastic in its attitude towards traditional institutions, and fiercely antagonistic to the privileges of foreigners founded on the 'unequal treaties'. The students of the 'new learning' inherited enough of the prestige belonging traditionally to the Confucian scholars to make them a very formidable force when they spoke with a common voice, and though there was no general agreement on problems of domestic reconstruction, there was unanimity on the need for freeing China from the servitudes on her sovereignty. Amid the strife of factions and the feuds, personal and provincial, which divided the nation, educated Chinese were everywhere becoming more and more 'nationality-conscious' and united in a demand for the revision of treaties and the recovery of China's full sovereign rights. So strong was the pressure of patriotic opinion that the most unprincipled of the military despots found it expedient to conform to the rule of the Kuomintang in relation to foreign policy. Long before Peking capitulated to Nationalist arms, its Foreign Office was adjusting Chinese diplomacy to the public opinion formed by Nationalist propaganda. The Chinese official delegations to the Paris Peace Conference in 1919 and to Washington in 1921 were in fact spokesmen of the Kuomintang, and put forward sweeping revisionist demands.

A new element was introduced into the situation when Sun Yat-sen on his return to Canton in 1923 brought with him the Russian Communist Borodin to be political adviser to the Canton Government. Thus began the four years partnership of the Kuomintang and the Communist International, a marriage of convenience in which each side hoped, first to make use of, and then to cheat, the other. The Kuomintang was primarily a party of the bourgeoisie; it was reformist and nationalist, but not Marxist. It aimed at reuniting China, at modernizing the civil administration and giving it a proper control over the army, at sweeping away the paraphernalia of an antiquated officialdom and liberating the productive forces of the country for the rapid development which was required for China's national resurgence—but all on sound capitalist lines. The dictatorship of the proletariat was the last thing desired by the bankers, merchants, and contractors who gave financial backing to the party. On the other hand, if the whole of China were to be won for the Kuomintang, it was necessary to obtain the

JACOB BORODIN

maximum of support from the masses by means of
a demagogic propaganda—in which they need fear
no competition from the military lords—and if they
were to have a prospect of success in a prolonged
war against the internationally recognized Government of Peking, they needed a measure of support
and assistance from abroad to set against the advantages which their foes derived from their legitimacy. Soviet Russia was ready to supply the aid
that was required to meet the situation.

From the Communist point of view support for
a bourgeois nationalist revolution was justified as a
policy likely to provide an opportunity for making a
truly proletarian revolution. The first task was to get
rid of 'feudalism'—the Chang Tso-lins, Wu P'ei-fus,
and the ex-monarchist bureaucrats—and for this purpose the Chinese bourgeoisie needed an alliance with
the masses of peasants and urban workers. The
Communist idea was to arrange this alliance for the
bourgeois leaders, hold to the coalition until victory
was won over the common enemy, and then at the
critical moment 'deepen the revolution', prevent the
bourgeoisie from consolidating its new class ascendancy, and make the transition from Kerensky to
Lenin. Further, Chinese nationalism could be used
as a weapon against the European capitalist Powers,
especially England. The power of finance-capital
imperialism could be undermined by an anti-imperialist league of the Soviet Union and the exploited colonial and semi-colonial peoples.

The Soviet Government was careful, however, not to enter into formal diplomatic relations with the Kuomintang rebels. The liaison with Canton was maintained through the Communist International (Comintern) and its branch, the newly formed Chinese Communist party. Official relations were maintained only with Peking, and Russian Communism as Soviet Government made treaties with the internationally recognized Government of China while Russian Communism as Comintern promoted the revolution against it. By Article 6 of the Sino-Soviet Treaty of 1924 each contracting party undertook not to permit within its borders the existence or activities of organizations subversive to the other party, and gave a pledge to abstain from hostile propaganda. But in the same year a large staff of Russian propaganda experts and military instructors were sent to Canton to help Borodin in reorganizing the Kuomintang and its army. The Chinese Communist party was affiliated to the Kuomintang, the left wing of the Kuomintang itself consisting of socialist intellectuals, and the Canton and Shanghai labour unions fell under Communist influence. The Russian experts remodelled the organization of the Kuomintang in the light of their own revolutionary experience. A new system of committees was built up, and the Government (the 'Political Council') was made directly responsible to the Central Executive Committee of the party. On the military side the Russian instructors headed by Galen (now, under the name of Blücher, commander of the Soviet Far Eastern Army and one of the five Marshals of the Soviet Union) set to work to provide the party with a picked fighting force of politically educated adherents to replace the mercenaries on whom Sun had hitherto relied. The nursery of the new model army was the Whampoa Military Academy, founded in 1924 with a hitherto obscure party supporter named Chiang Kai-shek as its Chinese principal. Chiang was not a Cantonese, but a native of Chekiang, and the nucleus of the new force was recruited from the disbanded army of the Anfu partisan Lu Yung-hsiang, who had been driven out of Chekiang by a general of the Chihli faction. Chiang was never on good terms with the Russian instructors, but he had to put up with them for the sake of the military training they were able to give. The Communists and their friends distrusted Chiang, but dared not get rid of him because of his conspicuous ability and popularity with the army.

At the end of 1924 Sun Yat-sen went north to negotiate with the Peking Government. He was already a sick man and died at Peking on March 12, 1925. He proved more valuable to his party dead than alive. He had been the supreme ideologist of the party, and his singleness of purpose had won for him the devotion of the zealots, but he had always lacked practical political competence. Chiang Kai-shek, on the other hand, was endowed with just those qualities in which Sun had been deficient, and it was

he who now became the dominant figure in the
party. Sun's teaching remained as an inspiration to
the faithful, but they were no longer embarrassed by
the blunders of his leadership. Sun dead became the
patron saint of the movement, his writings became
its Bible, and the ceremony of bowing to his portrait,
which was made a feature of all public gatherings
wherever the Kuomintang held power, gave a flavour
of religious devotion to party loyalty. Sunyacian-
ism went far to fill the void left by the disappearance
of Confucianism as a national orthodoxy. But for the
conduct of policy the mantle of Sun Yat-sen had
fallen on the shoulders of Chiang Kai-shek, a man of
temperament and outlook fundamentally different.
Sun was a doctrinaire democratic idealist who found
himself driven to resort to dictatorial rule, Chiang a
political schemer with all the instincts of an autocrat,
yet understanding much better than Sun the arts of
winning general support.

The first stroke of Chiang and his Whampoa
cadets after Sun's death was the liberation of Canton
from the horde of Yunnanese mercenaries which Sun
had imported to maintain himself in power. The
populace wreaked a terrible vengeance on the hated
'foreigners'. Canton was now in the possession of a
real Kuomintang army thirsting for revolutionary
conquests, and in the spring of 1926 Chiang launched
his famous 'Northern Expedition' over the passes
from Kwangtung into the basin of the Yangtse. The
expedition was a triumphal progress, and one pro-

vince after another passed into the hands of the
Nationalists. There was very little real fighting, for
the ground had been too well prepared by propaganda and intrigue. The civilian population, which
had suffered for years from the rapacity of military
despots, everywhere welcomed the invaders who
came with a programme of reforms, and the incurable
jealousies of the military factions and sub-factions
precluded the formation of a united front against
the politically disciplined Kuomintang forces. The
overlords of the Yangtse valley, Wu P'ei-fu and Sun
Ch'uan-fang, were deserted by subordinate com-
manders, who hastened to pass over to the side of the
Kuomintang, and the 'Christian General', Feng Yu-
hsiang, allied himself with the new power. Changsha
fell to the Nationalists on July 12, Hankow on September 7, Foochow on December 3, and Hangchow
on February 18, 1927. By the beginning of 1927
only two big factions remained in China—the Kuomintang and Chang Tso-lin's Fengtien military party,
which was based on Manchuria and now held Peking
with its Government of puppet officials. The rem-
nants of other factions rallied to one or other of these
groups. Fengtien forces took over what was left of
Sun Ch'uan-fang's domain on the lower Yangtse,
but they were defeated by the Nationalists, who occupied Shanghai (except for the foreign settlements) on
March 22 and Nanking two days later.

It was at this point that the ultimately inevitable rupture between Chiang Kai-shek and the

Communists took place, and it was decisive not only for China's domestic politics but also for her foreign relations. It was on the issue of anti-foreign agitation that the right and left wings of the Kuomintang were most sharply divided. The right wing was no less committed than the left to the cause of treaty revision, but it hoped to attain this end by unifying the country and acquiring a strength which foreign Powers would have to respect. As part of the process of national reorganization, however, it was essential to obtain credit facilities from the financial houses of Shanghai, and it was necessary, therefore, to avoid any acts of gross provocation against foreign persons and interests, though it was also necessary for the purposes of the civil war to work up to the utmost the nationalist revolutionary fervour on which the party hoped to ride to power. Unfortunately, it was not easy to combine the use of anti-foreign propaganda with a policy which would ultimately allow of a bargain with the magnates of credit, for the patriotic passions once aroused became too violent for the bourgeois politicians to manipulate. The Communists were not slow to take advantage of this situation ; it was to their interest to exacerbate the anti-imperialist conflict to the point at which no compromise would be possible. If Chiang were to strike a bargain with the Shanghai interests, the Kuomintang revolution would be stabilized on a bourgeois basis, and the Communists would be cold-shouldered. If, on the other hand, the Treaty Powers could be provoked into armed intervention, there would no longer be any room for a *moderate* nationalism, and in the stress and confusion of a new foreign invasion the Communists might find their opportunity to bring about an elemental mass uprising. It was also hoped that provocation by means of murders of foreigners and looting of foreign property would put the Treaty Powers, especially England and the U.S.A., in a very embarrassing position, for on the one side their nationals in China and the business interests involved would be furiously demanding intervention, while on the other there would be strong opposition to it from pacifist and anti-imperialist sections of opinion sympathetic to Chinese nationalist aspirations.

It was with the object of producing such a conflict and embroiling Chiang Kai-shek with the Treaty Powers that the left-wing extremists of the Kuomintang instigated the anti-foreign pogrom carried out by the troops under the command of Ho Yao-tsu after the capture of Nanking. Six foreigners were killed and a number wounded, and a crowd of refugees gathered on Socony Hill was only saved from massacre by a barrage of shell-fire put down by British and American warships on the Yangtse. All foreign property in the city was pillaged, including the consulates. The victims included British, American, French, Italian, and Japanese nationals. The attack bore every mark of deliberate preparation, for according to the evidence, which was afterwards carefully

sifted by official inquiries, the officers made no attempt
to put a stop to the outrages, and there was no general
sack of the city, the Nationalist troops being otherwise
well disciplined. This provocation naturally produced
acute tension, and it appears that a Communist outbreak in Shanghai was planned to follow the Nanking outrages. The International Settlement was
garrisoned by a British Defence Force of three bri-
gades of regular troops in addition to the Municipal
police and volunteer corps, but the vast city divided
between Chinese and foreign administration offered
a tempting opportunity for a terrorist campaign.
The General Labour Union was under Communist
influence, and on the evacuation of the Chinese-ad-
ministered parts of Shanghai by the Fengtien troops,
Communist gunmen seized the police stations. Three
soldiers of the Defence Force were killed by sniping,
but no general attack ever took place, for Chiang
Kai-shek hurried to Shanghai and took immediate
steps to crush the Communists. After bitter street-
fighting he succeeded in his object. Meanwhile the
left wing had gained control of the Nationalist Government, which had been shifted at the beginning of the
year from Canton to Hankow. Chiang countered by
setting up a new Government of his own adherents
at Nanking, and Hankow replied by dismissing him
from his post of Commander-in-Chief of the Kuomintang army. Civil war now broke out between
the two factions of the Kuomintang, while the war
against the Fengtien army was still in progress ; com-

plications were added by dissensions in both the Nanking and Hankow Governments. But the net result of the struggle in the spring and summer of 1927 was the discomfiture of the Communists, who were suppressed at Canton and Hankow as well as at Shanghai. The Russian advisers were expelled; Borodin left Hankow on July 27, and Galen followed a fortnight later. Previously the Peking Government, controlled by Chang Tso-lin, had produced a rupture of diplomatic relations with the Soviet Union by raiding Soviet premises and seizing documents which were held to prove the complicity of the Embassy in a Communist plot. In Russia the documents were denounced as forgeries, but in view of the resolutions passed by the Executive Committee of the Comintern at the end of 1926 there can be no doubt about the direction of Soviet policy at this time and the support given by Moscow to Communism in China. The publication of the documents had a considerable effect on the section of the Kuomintang which believed in co-operating with the Communists until Chang Tso-lin should be finally crushed.

The moderate element in the Kuomintang was further strengthened by the policy of the British Government which, while making a firm stand with its Defence Force in Shanghai, showed itself willing to make sacrifices of treaty rights—as in the surrender of the British Concession at Hankow—and refused to be drawn into any hasty military action

even after the Nanking outrages. The British diplomats were well aware that it was the aim of Borodin
to bring about hostilities between England and the
Chinese Nationalists, and they resolved to counter
anti-British intrigues by themselves entering into
diplomatic relations with the Nationalists. With the
arrival of the Nationalists on the Yangtse, the British
Foreign Office ceased to make a distinction between
legitimate and rebel authority in China, and instructed Mr. Lampson, the new Minister accredited
to the Peking Government, to go to Hankow and
negotiate with the Kuomintang. Lampson arrived
in Hankow on December 8, 1926; Borodin endeavoured to frustrate his mission by a furious anti-
British propaganda campaign with incitement to the
Hankow mob to attack the British Concession.[1] The
attack was made on January 3, 1927, but was held
off with bayonets by British marines and naval ratings,
who did not fire a single shot, though three of them
were wounded by missiles. As Sir Austen Chamberlain explained subsequently in the House of Com-
mons, 'it was a mob which you could not control
without firing, but our officers refrained from giving
the order to fire, in order not to create just that kind
of incident for which the mob had been provoked and
incited'. Soviet diplomacy was thus defeated by a
restraint which appeared to most British residents
in China at the time as abject weakness and inde-
cision. British policy was to win the confidence of

[1] See *Survey of Internat. Affairs, 1926*, pp. 346–50; *1927*, pp. 335–6.

the Kuomintang moderates and loosen the party's ties with the Comintern. The opportunity for a decisive move in carrying out this policy came in April 1927, when Chiang Kai-shek set up his right-wing Kuomintang Government at Nanking in opposition to the left-wing Kuomintang-Communist Government at Hankow. A British representative from the Peking Embassy had been stationed at Hankow since the beginning of the year, but when the Hankow group failed to give a satisfactory reply to a British note demanding reparation for the Nanking outrages, he was withdrawn, and provisional recognition was transferred to Nanking. Hankow was thus diplomatically isolated, and it was cut off also from contact with the Soviet Union, for Chiang's partisans held the south coast ports, and overland communications with Siberia were controlled by Feng Yu-hsiang, who joined Chiang in demanding the expulsion of Borodin and his staff. In these circumstances even the left-wing section of the Kuomintang turned against the Russians, and the Hankow Government broke up. After a period of confusion the various cliques and factions of the party reunited in support of a reconstructed Government at Nanking, and the Communists were left as a separate organization in armed revolt against Nationalist rule. Certain bodies of Kuomintang troops had been converted to Communism during the period of collaboration, and these forces now established themselves in mountainous districts, especially in the south of Kiangsi province, and set up local soviets. In December of 1927 a Communist column led by General Yeh Ting made a raid into Canton and raised the militant section of the proletariat in a bloody *émeute* which captured the city for four days. This episode resulted in an anti-Communist terror in South China, more severe than anything of the kind which had so far occurred, and in the closing of all Soviet consulates within the domain of the Kuomintang Government. It was now war to the knife between the Nationalists and their quondam allies. The Communist movement in the big cities was ruthlessly suppressed, and after their momentary occupation of Canton the Communists failed altogether to capture important centres of population, but they extended their hold on the country-side by raising the peasants against the landlords and seizing and redividing the land. Communism in China thus came more and more to be identified with an agrarian *jacquerie,* and the Chinese Soviet Republic which it set up was a loose federation of scattered areas of peasant revolt sustained by elusive guerrilla bands operating from mountain strongholds.

The struggle for power within the Kuomintang having been settled for the time being by the end of 1927, the war against Chang Tso-lin and his vassals was renewed. Feng Yu-hsiang, who held the provinces of Honan, Shensi, and Kansu, and Yen Hsi-shan, the ruler of Shansi, fought as adherents of the Kuomintang, so that forces owing at least nominal

CHINA'S JACQUES BONHOMME
A typical peasant

allegiance to the Nanking Government closed in on Peking both from the south and from the west. Peking was finally captured by General Yen, whose troops marched in on June 8, 1928. With the fall of the old capital the Nationalists succeeded to the legitimacy which had belonged to Peking Governments ever since the beginning of the civil wars; they did not, however, move their own Government from Nanking, for it had been decided to make Nanking the future capital. The Peking Foreign Office was closed, and the conduct of China's foreign affairs was taken over by the Nationalist Government which was now formally recognized as the legal Government of China by foreign nations.

The status of Manchuria, however, still remained in doubt after the capture of Peking by the Nationalists, and it was in Manchuria that the 'rights recovery' revisionist campaign of the Kuomintang was to reach its tragic climax. Chinese revisionism assumed a new form north of the Great Wall, because it had there to deal with 'special interests' and no longer with treaty rights common to the majority of the important foreign Powers. The treaty rights which Chinese nationalism was striving to abrogate fell under five heads: extraterritoriality, autonomous settlements, tariff restriction, leased territories, and railway zones. The first three kinds of privilege were shared by all the nations enjoying most-favoured-nation treatment, and there was therefore likely to be a united front of these states (notably England, France, the

U.S.A., and Japan) in resistance to any high-handed action against their common rights. Leased territories were now held by three nations only: by England (Hong Kong New Territory), by France (Kwangchow-wan), and by Japan (Kwantung).[1] These were places with garrisons and could only be taken by open warfare. Railway zones, on the other hand, were only possessed by two nations—Soviet Russia and Japan—and with full privilege only by Japan, so that there was no bloc of nations with an interest in the defence of such rights, and Russia and Japan could not easily show a united front for the purpose because of the mutual hostility and suspicion which had divided them ever since the days of Japan's Siberian expedition.

The two railway zones of Manchuria—those of the C.E.R. and S.M.R.—were the legacies of the Russian quasi-conquest of Manchuria between 1896 and 1904. Only the Japanese retained all the privileges of the original system, including the right to maintain troops as railway guards throughout their zone. The Russian rights had been reduced by the treaties of 1924, but enough remained to make the C.E.R. something more than merely a commercial railway company. The line ran into Russian territory at both ends and was really part of the Trans-Siberian system; it was under the control, not of a private company, but of the Russian state, and this control had been made by trickery

---

[1] England restored Weihaiwei to China after Japan's restoration of the former German leasehold of Kiaochow.

much more effective than the Chinese signatories of the 1924 treaties had meant it to be. It had been agreed that the General Manager was to be a Soviet citizen, but he was to be supervised by a Board of Directors on which Russians and Chinese were equally represented. The Russian Directors, however, stultified the arrangement by failing to appear at Board meetings, so that it was impossible to form a quorum, and the Russian Manager was left with unhampered power. An unsuccessful attempt to liquidate the C.E.R. establishment had been made by Chang Tso-lin in January 1936, after the General Manager Ivanov had obstructed the transit of his troops in a local civil war between Chang and a rebellious subordinate named Kuo Sun-ling. The Japanese at that time had made an equally political use of *their* railway by forbidding Kuo's troops to cross it; Soviet Russia and Japan were in fact backing Kuo and Chang respectively for the supremacy in Manchuria. Chang emerged victorious from the conflict, and proceeded to avenge himself by arresting Ivanov and three of the Russian Directors and lodging them in prison. Soviet Russia had met this challenge with a three-days ultimatum demanding the release of the arrested men and the immediate restoration of normal traffic on the railway; the threat of force was sufficient, and Chang gave way.

Chang Tso-lin, as long as he ruled Manchuria, was continually on bad terms with the Soviet Union, but was fairly well disposed towards the Japanese,

HH

who gave him support in various ways. The Kuomintang influence on the other hand was both anti-Soviet (since the break with the Communists in 1927) and anti-Japanese. Chinese nationalism nursed a special resentment against Japan because of the Twenty-one Demands. The original lease of the railway transferred to Japan by the Treaty of Portsmouth expired in 1923, but it had been extended by one of the treaties Japan extorted from China in 1915, and the S.M.R. as the beneficiary of China's most recent humiliation was for Chinese patriots the most hateful of all foreign institutions within the borders of China.

In view of the pronounced anti-Japanese sentiments of the Kuomintang, Japan had an obvious interest in preserving the independent rule of the friendly Chang Tso-lin in Manchuria. The Seiyukai Cabinet of General Baron Tanaka, which was in power in Japan in 1927–9, sought to keep the Kuomintang at a safe distance from Manchuria by impeding the advance of the Nationalists from the lower Yangtse towards Peking. A Japanese expeditionary force was sent to Shantung to protect the lives and properties of the numerous Japanese subjects residing in the province, and after what had happened at Nanking in March 1927 it was difficult for any nation but China to take exception to its presence. However, it also served as an obstacle in the path of the Kuomintang march to the north. Fighting broke out in May 1928 between Japanese and Chinese Nationalist troops at Tsinan, the provincial capital of Shantung. The Japanese force routed its opponents and occupied Tsinan, forbidding any further Nationalist movement along the railway from Nanking to Peking. The blocking of the advance from the south did not, however, remove the threat to Peking from the west, and when it became clear that Chang Tso-lin was hard pressed by the Shansi army, the Japanese Government made a new move. It announced both to the Peking and Nanking Governments that 'if the situation should become so menacing as to threaten the peace and order of Manchuria, the Japanese Government . . . might possibly be constrained to take appropriate and effective steps for the maintenance of peace and order in Manchuria'. This meant that the Japanese were resolved to intercept the Peking–Mukden railway in the narrow coastal pass between the mountains and the sea at Shanhaikwan. Chang was warned to take his army back to Manchuria while it was still intact, as it would not be allowed through the Japanese cordon if it came as a vanquished force with victorious Kuomintang troops at its heels. Chang obeyed this order and evacuated Peking without fighting, but it seems that he resented the Japanese dictation and would have preferred to risk a battle with the Shansi army. On leaving Peking he went straight to Mukden, and as his train was passing under the bridge by which the S.M.R. crossed the Peking–Mukden line it was blown up by a mine. The authors and motives of this assassination remain to this day extremely obscure, but it seems probable that Chang's Chief of Staff, General Yang Yu-ting, had a hand in it and that certain Japanese officials in Manchuria were privy to the plot.[1] It may be surmised that the motive of the Japanese accomplices was to forestall a *rapprochement* between Chang Tso-lin and Chiang Kai-shek. The latter had twice made overtures to the former for an alliance, but the Manchurian dictator, confident of his own strength, had rejected them; now, after the loss of Peking, he was in a chastened mood, and ready to consider a new orientation of policy. Yang Yu-ting, on the other hand, was alleged to be in favour of the complete separation of Manchuria from China Proper—in fact, of a Manchukuo. The conspirators may have thought that Chang Tso-lin's heir, his son Chang Hsüeh-liang, would be incapable of taking over his father's authority and that effective power would be held by Yang. However, the young Chang at once assumed the autocracy as by dynastic right and showed that he had a will of his own. Japan made strenuous efforts to prevent him from striking a bargain with the Nanking Government, but all to no purpose. He negotiated with Nanking with separatism as a bargaining lever and made an agreement which gave him a finger in the pie of Chinese national politics without impairing in essentials his independence in

---

[1] For an account of debates in the Japanese Diet on 'a grave Manchurian Incident' see T. Takeuchi, *War and Diplomacy in the Japanese Empire*, pp. 275–82.

Manchuria. He was appointed one of the sixteen State Councillors at Nanking and confirmed in the administration of the three Manchurian provinces plus Jehol; in return he hoisted the Kuomintang flag in Manchuria and admitted branches of the party to legal existence there. On January 10, 1929, he completed his emancipation from pro-Japanese restraint by the murder of Yang Yu-ting, who was shot down at a reception to which Chang Hsüeh-liang had invited him.

XII

MANCHUKUO

WITH the formal reunification of China Proper and Manchuria under a Government of the Kuomintang party, Manchuria became once more a storm-centre of international relations. The typhoon which had started from Canton had swept northward over China following closely the track of the T'ai P'ing rebellion seventy years before, and having passed successively over Hankow, Nanking, and Peking, moved at the end of 1928 into Manchuria and acquired there a new vigour and destructiveness. In 1929, just as the relations between the authorities of China and the other foreign Powers were ceasing to be unduly strained, the Kuomintang in the person of Chang Hsüeh-liang was embarking on a new phase of struggle against Soviet Russia and Japan in Manchuria, and this was destined to have more far-reaching international repercussions than the earlier phase of the movement within China Proper.

The problems of treaty revision relating to China Proper were not indeed such as to give rise to a really critical situation. The servitudes on Chinese sovereignty outside Manchuria were either of a kind on which the Treaty Powers were prepared to negotiate for revision—such as tariff restrictions and extra-territoriality—or else were a common interest of so many nations—such as the autonomy of the International Settlement at Shanghai—that they were virtually immune from revisionist pressure. The most serious international aspect of the Kuomintang movement in the years 1925–7 had not been its demand for the revision of the 'unequal treaties', but its alliance with the Comintern, which had threatened the capitalist Great Powers with a Bolshevik China. This danger had been averted by Chiang Kai-shek's suppression of the Communists in the cities under Nationalist control in 1927, and the Powers, who had been thoroughly frightened by the prospect of an extension of the Soviet Union to the South China Sea, were ready to allow diplomatic gains to their deliverer on issues which were not regarded as vital. The diplomats of the Powers were aware that Chiang Kai-shek was no doctrinaire fanatic, but that he had to consider the public opinion of his party which required him to be high-handed and intransigent. They were disposed to give him a certain latitude for irregular unilateral action with regard to the treaties and not to insist too strongly on the letter of the law. This policy was a wise one where vital interests were not involved, but the general weakening of respect for treaties and contracts was bound to have serious effects on the conduct of diplomacy in a crisis. Typical of the treaty-repudiation tactics of the Nanking Government was a decree issued in 1929 unilaterally abrogating the extraterritorial privileges of foreigners in China as from January 1930. The Powers concerned were willing to negotiate on the question, but declined to recognize the validity of such a unilateral denunciation, and when the appointed time came no action on the decree was taken by the Chinese authorities. On the other hand, the decree was not withdrawn and no pressure was put on the Chinese Government for its formal cancellation. The Powers in fact accepted, or at least did not vigorously condemn, a number of unilateral treaty repudiations on the part of China, and the yielding to 'revolutionary diplomacy' led in a couple of years to a situation in which a victim of systematic treaty violations was tempted to appeal to force to secure certain rights and by the logic of military victory went far beyond the original rights which had been disputed.

The railway zones of the C.E.R. and S.M.R. were, as we have seen, the special targets of Kuomintang revisionism after 1928: because their politico-economic ascendancy over large areas of Chinese territory was particularly obnoxious to Chinese sovereignty; because they were not common interests of the Treaty Powers, but concerned only Russia and Japan who were not on good terms with each other; and because Soviet Russia and Japan held the first two places in the Kuomintang's scale of dislike for foreign states, the former because of its connexion with Communism (now the implacable enemy of the definitely bourgeois Kuomintang) and the latter because of the never-to-be-forgiven Twenty-one Demands. On the other hand, the C.E.R. and the S.M.R. were both vital interests of the countries to which they belonged, the former because it was Soviet Russia's direct line of communication with Vladivostok through the Manchurian salient, and the latter because of the great amount of capital which had been sunk in the railway, its branches and its subsidiary enterprises, forming one of the main factors in the scheme of Japan's national economy. Add to the importance of these interests the fact that the Governments of both Russia and Japan were directly involved in the ownership and administration of their respective railways, and it is clear that in 1929 the stage was set in Manchuria for a conflict much more acute than any which had so far occurred in the course of China's Nationalist revolution.

The first attack was delivered against the C.E.R. On the pretext that the Russian organization of the railway was being used for purposes of Communist propaganda and intrigue, the Manchurian authorities, on instructions from Chang Hsüeh-liang, repeated the coup of 1926 on a larger scale, forcibly taking over the telegraph and telephone system of the railway, occupying Soviet premises, arresting two hundred Soviet Russian employees of the railway (including the General Manager) and virtually expropriating the Soviet interest in the Company. The reply of the Soviet Union to this challenge was to concentrate troops on the Siberian frontier, and

after the break-down of negotiations for a settlement
to conduct military raids into Manchuria, attacking
and punishing the Chinese forces near the border
without making a permanent occupation of territory.
These tactics of undeclared war proved extremely
effective, and after his troops had been heavily
defeated and driven out of Manchuli and Hailar
in November 1929, Chang Hsüeh-liang gave up
the struggle and submitted unconditionally to the
Russian demands, restoring the *status quo ante* on
the C.E.R. and dropping his complaints about the
propaganda activity of the Company's institutions.
This triumph for the Soviet was won by the use of
military force and by nothing else. Moves made by
other Powers to mediate in the dispute were firmly
rejected by the Soviet Government, which insisted
that the quarrel must be settled by direct negotiation between the Soviet Union and China without
any interference by third parties. Soviet Russia was
not a member of the League of Nations, and it was
therefore useless to bring the case to Geneva—though
theoretically China had a remedy under Article 17
of the Covenant, which provides for sanctions
against a state not a member of the League. Russia
had signed the Kellogg Pact 'renouncing war as an
instrument of national policy' only the year before,
and several of the co-signatories called her attention
to the fact, but the Soviet Government refused to
listen to these remonstrances and maintained that
its military invasions of Chinese territory were in

GALEN *alias* BLÜCHER
Marshal of the Soviet Union and commander of the Soviet Far Eastern Army

self-defence. As the Chinese had not penetrated into Russian territory, but had only taken action, however provocative and high-handed it may have been, within their own borders, the Soviet contention could only mean that any war in support of property claims in another country was an act of self-defence, and the Kellogg Pact was thus exposed as an empty form even before it had yet been ratified by all its signatories.

The ambitious dictator of Manchuria was preoccupied during the following year (1930) with a new internal conflict which had broken out in China Proper, this time between Chiang Kai-shek and his former allies in the advance on Peking—Generals Feng Yu-hsiang and Yen Hsi-shan. Chang sent an army south of the Great Wall to help Chiang and drove Yen's army out of Peking. While this civil war was being fought out, China's foreign policy was allowed to drift to such an extent that, as Professor Toynbee remarked in his *Survey of International Affairs for 1930*, 'the history of the relations between China and foreign Powers—both the Treaty Powers and the U.S.S.R.—was less eventful in 1930 than in any previous year since January 1920'. It was the calm before the storm. In 1931 Chang Hsüeh-liang, encouraged by his successful campaign south of the Wall and anxious to increase his prestige with the Kuomintang by some exploit in 'rights recovery', began to harry the Japanese interests in South Manchuria, while simultaneously a chain of events in world economy plunged Japan into an acute domestic crisis and led to a rapid re-emergence of the military-chauvinist faction which had been out of favour in that country since 1920.

The Chinese Nationalist idea in South Manchuria was to strangle the S.M.R. system and make it unprofitable by means of a competing system of Chinese lines based on a new port at Hulutao on the Chihli Gulf, and also by evasion and obstruction of various treaty provisions on which the activities of the S.M.R. depended. The new anti-Japanese railway system was to be financed largely by defaults on debts owed to the S.M.R. for lines which had been constructed with capital advanced by the S.M.R. The failure to make payments on these loans was part of a regular practice whereby the Japanese were made to provide the capital for their own discomfiture. Diplomatic protests were of no avail, and a whole series of treaty obligations were ignored or evaded in accordance with the aim of driving the S.M.R. into liquidation. Chang Hsüeh-liang had no intention of attacking the railway zone and its Japanese army garrisons in open warfare, but he appears to have supposed that he was quite safe from Japanese retaliation within his own territory and that the 'conciliation diplomacy' of Baron Shidehara was good for any strain that could be placed on it. He did not realize how much he was contributing to the force of the militarist reaction which was about to break loose in Japan.

Japan may be said to have suffered the worst evils of the world economic depression, which began at the end of 1929, without ever having enjoyed the boom of 1924–9. Japan's economic system, lopsided and precariously founded at the best of times, had received a terrific blow from the great earthquake which devastated Tokyo and Yokohama in 1923, and she had to spend the next six years recuperating from the great disaster. Then, just as prosperity appeared to be returning, the world slump banished all such hopes and brought the nation face to face with an appalling economic crisis. The extent of the collapse may be gauged from the fact that the value of Japan's export trade fell from 2,100 million yen in 1929 to 1,430 million in 1930 and 1,118 million in 1931. Japan's main raw material export, raw silk, was particularly hard hit,[1] for the luxury industry which it served was one of the first to feel the impact of the slump. Socially and politically the catastrophic fall of silk prices had a most serious effect, for silk production had been the extra economic activity which enabled the peasants all over Japan just to pay their rents and taxes and make ends meet. With the collapse of the silk market the overcrowded country-side was afflicted with an acute economic crisis involving both the peasants and the landowning gentry. The situation was aggravated by the fact that Japan, having been

[1] Raw silk exports from Japan to U.S.A. in 1929, $348,229,000; in 1930, $196,925,000.

driven off the gold standard during the financially
unstable post-earthquake period, had returned to
monetary respectability (as the gold standard was
then regarded) in the summer of 1929, thus sub-
jecting the national economy to severe deflationary
pressure just at the very moment when it was about
to be overtaken by the world slump. The Minseito
party, which had put Japan back on the gold standard, had to assume responsibility for a financial
stringency which was painful in 1929 and had become intolerable by 1931. The landlords who received rents in kind and the debt-burdened small
business men clamoured for an inflationary policy,
and their cause was championed by the Seiyukai
whose monetary unorthodoxy came to be the height
of fashion after the pound sterling had gone off gold.

The ruin of the silk trade and the intensity of the
deflation were together sufficient to fill up Japan's
cup of troubles. There were added to them the sky-
high Smoot-Hawley tariff which came into effect
in the United States in June 1930, the 'squeezing-
out' pressure applied against the S.M.R. and its
enterprises in Manchuria, and in July 1931 a new
anti-Japanese boycott proclaimed by the Chinese
Chambers of Commerce at Shanghai and elsewhere
on account of the Wanpaoshan incident and its
sequel in Korea.[1]

The accumulation of disasters which fell upon

[1] For the details of this incident and the riots in Korea see the
Lytton Report, p. 61.

Japan in the *annus terribilis* 1931 was politically fatal to the Minseito Cabinet, to its deflationism (represented by Finance Minister Inouye), and to its 'conciliation diplomacy' (represented by Foreign Minister Shidehara). The financial and foreign policies of the Minseito were closely connected; the party served the big banking and heavy industrial interests, which were anxious to maintain favourable conditions for borrowing abroad and demanded therefore financial 'soundness' and good diplomatic relations with London and Washington. The strong or 'positive' policy towards China, advocated by the Seiyukai, was condemned by Minseito partisans on the ground that it would involve an increase in military expenditure, would damage export trade by provoking Chinese boycotts, and would lead to conflicts with England and the United States. Idealists supported the Minseito with the argument that Japan had treated China harshly in the past and must now show patience and restraint in order to win her goodwill. It was held that nothing worth while could be achieved by violence, but that a policy of conciliation would pay in the end. The spokesman of this school of thought was Baron Shidehara, who won his spurs diplomatically at the Washington Conference and was Foreign Minister from 1924 to 1927 and again from 1929 to 1931. He was still in office in the autumn of 1931 when the direction of ʟoreign policy was wrenched out of his hands by the action of the Army.

The Seiyukai politicians had had a chance to show the virtues of their 'positive policy' when they were in power in 1927-9, but it was generally agreed that the ministry of General Baron Tanaka (who was both Premier and Foreign Minister) had been a failure. His dispatch of troops to Shantung had involved a prolonged and costly occupation with no satisfactory result; the attempt to keep the Kuomintang out of Peking and Manchuria had been unsuccessful, and the most obvious effects of Tanaka's vigour had been another anti-Japanese boycott and a flare-up of anti-Japanese feeling in China. The Minseito partisans drew the moral that the positive policy was a path of short-sighted folly and that it could only make a bad matter worse. In extreme chauvinist circles, however, the very opposite conclusion was reached; it was held that Tanaka had failed to achieve anything because he had not been forceful *enough*, because he had paid too much regard to criticism in the Diet and adverse comments in England and America. The Japanese militarists declared that Tanaka had been too timid, and that he ought to have dealt with Chang Hsüeh-liang by the methods of ultimatum and military action which Soviet Russia had used so effectively in the autumn of 1929.

The swing of Japanese opinion towards a chauvinist policy in 1931 was accentuated by the disappointment of the classes specially associated with the Minseito at the fruits of Shidehara diplomacy. The big banks and heavy industry capitalists were deeply involved in S.M.R. enterprises and began to take alarm at Chang's 'squeezing-out' policy, while the textile manufacturers who had supported the conciliation policy as a cure for boycotts were thoroughly disillusioned when the Chinese started a new boycott over the Wanpaoshan affair, and reflected that Japanese trade could not be more than boycotted if Japanese armies traversed China from end to end.

Still more dangerous to the Minseito Cabinet was the conflict of its civilian members with both the fighting services—not only with the Army, which was always anti-Minseito in temper, but also with the Navy, which had Minseito political connexions. The Cabinet secured the ratification of the London Naval Treaty of 1930 in the teeth of strong opposition from the Admiralty. The Navy Minister, Admiral Takarabe, approved of the Treaty, but it was denounced by the Navy Chief of Staff, Admiral Kato, who resigned after he had failed to get his view adopted. The service was indignant at the stubborn resolve of the civilian Prime Minister Hamaguchi to overrule Kato's opposition, for it was held in Navy circles that the 'prerogative of supreme command' belonging constitutionally to the Emperor meant that the Chief of Staff, and not the Prime Minister, was the proper person to advise the Emperor on a question of requirements for national defence. The logic of Minseito liberalism, however, certainly implied the subordination of the fighting services to the authority of the Cabinet, and the dispute over the

London Naval Treaty only brought to a head a constitutional conflict which had long been developing. What was disastrous for the Minseito ministry was the fact that the crisis in its relations with the Navy coincided in time with the rapid deterioration of economic conditions and the increase of social unrest which gave an opportunity to all the enemies of liberalism. Public opinion supported the Cabinet in its struggle with the Admiralty in 1930, but in 1931 the Minseito Government found itself confronted with the hostility of the services while the tide of popular favour was ebbing away from it. The Army now began to come to the fore; it turned a deaf ear to suggestions that it should assist in balancing the budget by consenting to cuts in military expenditure, and began to conduct a campaign of propaganda in favour of 'direct action' in Manchuria. In March the police uncovered a conspiracy of army officers to overthrow the Government by a *coup d'état*, and the War Minister, General Minami, was suspected of complicity. Wakatsuki, who had succeeded Hamaguchi as Minseito leader and Prime Minister, did not dare to get rid of Minami, though the latter publicly attacked the Cabinet of which he was a member. In August he addressed a conference of generals and roundly denounced Baron Shidehara for the weakness of his policy towards China; his speech was published to the great embarrassment of the Foreign Minister.

Such was the state of affairs in Japan on the eve

of the Mukden Incident of September 18 which was radically to change the course of events in the Far East. With the capture of Mukden the Japanese Army took the offensive on two fronts—against Chang Hsüeh-liang in Manchuria and against liberalism within Japan. The Minseito Cabinet remained in office until the second week of December, and its civilian members did their best to restrain the Army from irrevocable commitments in Manchuria. But it was fighting a losing battle ; a storm of patriotic enthusiasm swept the country and under the stress of war fever the Minseito party split in two. The Wakatsuki ministry resigned before the year was out, and the Seiyukai was called to power. The new Government put Japan off the gold standard on the day after it took office and gave full rein to the Army in Manchuria. On January 4, 1932, Japanese troops occupied Shanhaikwan, where the Great Wall of China running along the mountain crests ends on the sea-coast, and thus by force of arms divided Manchuria from China-within-the-Wall. Nine months later Japan formally recognized a Japanese-occupied Manchuria as a separate sovereign state under the name of Manchukuo.

XIII

CONCLUSION

THE course of events since the beginning of the Japanese military drive in Manchuria in 1931 belongs to 'contemporary' history and is fresh in the memory of every one who has taken an interest in international affairs during the last seven years. It would be superfluous, therefore, to continue the narrative up to the present day without an abundance of detail impossible in such a brief study as this. But a survey of the Far Eastern situation at the beginning of 1939 should enable us to trace certain main lines of development whereby we may see current events in their historical perspective. The crisis of 1931 opened a new chapter in the relations of states in the Far East, but the principal characters and the plot in which they act are still those with which we have become familiar in the chapters preceding.

We have seen that from the beginning of the twentieth century up to the time of the Washington Conference England and the United States with their great maritime commercial interests in the Far East steadily opposed moves made by either Russia or Japan to obtain paramountcy over China. From 1895 to 1905 the initiative lay with Russia, and her progress appeared to be beyond the reach of Anglo-American interference. Backed by French money and aided by the benevolent neutrality of Germany, Russia's Far Eastern empire grew in strength. Considering only the Western Powers, the German Kaiser was right when he declared that nothing could stop the Russians from marching to Peking as soon as they had completed their preparations. But Japan, covered by an alliance with England, challenged Russia to a military contest on the mainland and defeated her. The Treaty of Portsmouth left Japan firmly established in Korea and South Manchuria, intercepting the main road from Siberia to China, and Russia decisively headed off from her ultimate objective, though still retaining an extensive 'sphere' in North Manchuria and Outer Mongolia.

It soon became clear that Japan herself had aspirations to that hegemony which she had prevented Russia from acquiring. But Japan had to proceed cautiously. Her expansion on the Continent was no more welcome to England and the United States than Russia's had been, and she was much more accessible to their displeasure. She was an insular nation and was vulnerable to superior sea-power, as Russia was not. Even more compelling a circumstance, she was financially weak and dependent on the Anglo-Saxon Powers who had been her backers in 1904; she could not flout them to a point at which strained relations would endanger her fragile economic structure. These two fundamental conditions of policy explain the comparative insignificance of Japan's net gains on the mainland between 1905 and 1931. She was able to do a little empire-building by taking advantage of England's European preoccupations, especially in the four years 1914–18, but after the war she had to disgorge a great part of what she had swallowed. At Washington a new curb was put on her ambitions by the Nine-Power Treaty, and during the next few years it seemed that the maintenance of good relations with England and the U.S.A. had become a *sine qua non* of Japanese foreign policy, precluding any further adventures in imperialism.

The Japanese action in 1931 involved, nevertheless, an uncompromising defiance of the Anglo-American combine, and revealed a new strength in Japan's position. Her relative power had in fact been increasing since the Washington Conference. The Washington Naval Treaty safeguarded Japan against the strengthening of American naval bases west of Hawaii or of British north of Singapore, and the halt to competition in the building of capital ships (which Japan could least afford) was turned to advantage in the unrestricted categories. Edwin A. Falk in his biography of Admiral Togo[1] has admirably summed up the process of Japan's emancipation from Anglo-Saxon tutelage:

'Between the Conferences of Washington (1921–22) and London (1930), the United States, with a per capita wealth seven times greater than Japan's, expended upon new warcraft (laid down and completed) less than one-seventh as much per capita. At Washington in 1921 Kato was confronted by an American fleet, built and

---

[1] *Togo and the Rise of Japanese Sea-Power*, p. 446.

building under the 1916 programme and the exigencies of the war, vastly greater than his own, and Japan's lesser resources rendered competitive construction a forlorn hope. During the ensuing decade the seemingly impossible came to pass. By the time of Togo's death [1934] the Japanese fleet, although numerically inferior in capital ships, had units in that category that on the average were swifter and perhaps stronger, had substantial equality in aircraft carriers and heavy cruisers, and had an actual preponderance in light cruisers, under-age destroyers and submarines. How could such an absolute control of home waters have failed to stimulate the undeviating Japanese Imperial programme into activity before the advantage should be lost?'

The American fleet in 1932 would have been by itself quite incapable of coping with the Japanese in the Western Pacific. It had in any case no base for capital ships west of Hawaii. The British navy had no battle-fleet base east of Malta at that time; the Singapore base, on which work had been more than once held up owing to hopes of general disarmament, was not yet ready. These strategic conditions gave Japan (with her navy operating from the homeland battle-fleet bases of Yokosuka, Kure, and Sasebo) a definite supremacy in Asiatic waters from Kamchatka to Luzon, and would have enabled her in case of need, not only to assure her own communications with the mainland, but also to impose a blockade on the entire coastline of China. The British and American navies, even if combined, were not in a position to offer battle in the China

Seas, and could only make war on Japan by long-distance blockade from Hawaii.

Financially, Japan proved to be able to fend for herself and to be no longer controllable by ordinary economic pressure. She had come of age as an industrialized nation, though her economy was still backward in many respects on account of its hasty development and artificial specialization for purposes of national war-power. She was no longer dependent on European and American goodwill to the extent to which she had been hitherto. She was indeed in a desperate economic plight in 1931 as a consequence of the world depression, and it was widely believed in England and America that the extra expenditure imposed by the Manchurian venture and general war preparations would reduce her to bankruptcy without the application of any formal sanctions by the League of Nations. Those who believed that angels watched over the Covenant of the League and would punish transgressors without risk to its earthly guarantors consoled themselves with the thought that Japan would be compelled very soon to come to Geneva as a suppliant and beg for a loan on any terms that the outraged League might see fit to impose. But Japan obstinately refused to go bankrupt; instead of capitulating to an empty purse Japan followed England off the gold standard and kept herself in funds by a world-wide trade drive conducted with state co-ordination as a great national enterprise. A depreciated currency, an extreme concentration of finance capital control, and an abundance of cheap labour due to the impoverishment of the countryside enabled Japan to penetrate markets everywhere and accompany her territorial conquests on the mainland of East Asia with a general commercial expansion of unprecedented magnitude. It is true that this trade boom did not appreciably relieve the distress of the masses—which was indeed the condition of the success in foreign markets—but it enabled Japan to maintain essential imports and to stock war materials on a large scale.

This trade would have been cut off if the League States, supported by the U.S.A., had applied full economic sanctions against Japan. But League sanctions would have put Japan in a state of siege, and it is very unlikely that she would have either surrendered at the outset or passively awaited defeat by slow economic attrition. She would probably have replied to sanctions by formally declaring war on China and imposing a strict blockade on Chinese ports; this would mean that the sanctionist Powers during a period of intense trade depression, when exporting interests everywhere were trying desperately to hold on to dwindling markets, would cut themselves off from virtually all their trade with *both* Japan *and* China—unless they could break the blockade of China by force, and that, for the reasons already given, they had little hope of being able to do. Inasmuch as Japan and the Western maritime Powers were inaccessible to each other for purposes of direct attack, a war between them must have taken the form of a double blockade—a short-range blockade of China by Japan and a long-range blockade of Japan by the Western Powers. If such a contest had been prolonged to the bitter end, Japan would certainly have had to capitulate, for her whole economy must have been ruined. But the economic strain on the sanctionist nations would have been considerable and the will to carry on the struggle *à outrance* would have been far less than in Japan, even if the initial step of imposing sanctions had been taken by the governments concerned. For Japan Manchuria was certainly by the traditional canons of diplomacy a region of 'vital interest'; it was not so either for Britain or the U.S.A. The urge in those countries towards the application of sanctions was almost entirely an expression of idealism, of attachment to the new international order supposed to have been created by the League Covenant and the Pact of Paris. It was an emotional enthusiasm without any ground of immediate national interest; it was generally ill-informed as to the likely consequences of the actions it sought to promote; it derived its force from the political Left and was at its weakest in the most influential circles of industry and finance. But to be effective in great international conflicts idealism requires an alloy of baser metal; devotion to abstract principles must be reinforced by awareness of a direct threat to national security or main economic interests, if a country is to endure for long the sacrifices required in a war of attrition. This condition was not fulfilled either in Britain or America with regard to the Manchurian issue, and if these Powers had tried to coerce Japan into withdrawal by means of sanctions, it seems probable that business interests would have pressed their governments into a compromise settlement with Japan long before Japan was driven to the point of surrender. It may be argued that international order would have been better served by such a compromise than by the policy of inactivity which was actually followed; compromise, however, which is a virtue as between litigants, is no way of asserting the reign of law—a tribunal is not vindicated if the judge has to bargain with the accused.

The U.S.A., not being a member of the League of Nations, was not bound by any treaty obligation to apply sanctions, and the outcry against Japan arose mainly from the established pro-Chinese sentiment in the country. In response to the pressure of public opinion, Washington was ready to go a long way in diplomatic opposition to Japan's course, but it does not appear from Mr. Stimson's own account of his policy that any really coercive action was contemplated. Britain, on the other hand, who was theoretically bound to apply Article 16 of the League Covenant if Japan were declared the aggressor at Geneva, fell short of America in willingness for diplomatic intervention. The British 'National' Government, which took office just before

the Mukden Incident, was composed mainly of men
who were indifferent or hostile towards the League
of Nations idea, and this negative attitude gave
scope to two factors of policy which worked in favour
of Japan : European pre-occupation and fear of
Communism.

The greatest advantage to Britain from the Anglo-
Japanese alliance in the years 1907–18 had been its
effect in enabling the Admiralty to concentrate the
British navy in European waters instead of having
to keep a large part of it stationed in the Pacific
with an entirely separate system of bases and supplies. After the termination of the Alliance it was
still hoped that the need for a separate battle-fleet
in the Pacific could be avoided through friendship
with Japan ; good relations with Tokyo were felt to
be the best security for the vulnerable British possessions and interests in the Far East. Britain was
therefore extremely reluctant to provoke the resentment of Japan by thwarting her on a crucial issue,
and there was a strong disposition to tolerate Japanese
expansion in the direction where it was least damaging to British interests. The Americans were less
influenced by considerations of this kind, because
they were quite ready (up to last year) to keep their
whole navy in the Pacific.

Dislike of Communism was a sentiment common
to the governments both of Britain and of the U.S.A.,
but it operated more powerfully as a policy-shaping
factor in London than in Washington. British capital

had suffered far more than American from Bolshevik repudiation and confiscation in Russia, and had been much more deeply involved in the anti-Bolshevik interventions of 1918–20; further, Britain had been singled out as the special target of Communist propaganda in China in 1925–7, and the unrest in India made her government very nervous at the prospect of an increase of Soviet power and prestige anywhere in Asia. Though the immediate danger of Communism in China had been removed in 1927, there remained several nuclei of Communist military power in the interior of the country, and the most important of them—the Soviet territory in Kiangsi— was dangerously close to Nanking. The collapse of Japanese power on the mainland—which might occur if Japan suffered a great humiliation in foreign policy and then broke up internally through civil dissension—might well bring about an ascendancy of Soviet influence in Manchuria and Inner Mongolia leading to a revival of Communism in China Proper. Such developments could not be a matter for exact calculation, but it was vaguely felt that any serious weakening of Japan involved an increased risk of Communist penetration of the Far East, and that a Japanese military occupation of a territory which had already for two decades been regarded as their sphere of influence was less disturbing to the Far Eastern balance of power than an attempt to coerce Japan was likely to be. No mere restoration of the *status quo* would be possible once a major war had begun in the Far East; Japan must win or be broken. There was therefore the possibility that a struggle undertaken to vindicate the League Covenant and restore Manchuria to Chinese sovereignty might serve instead to clear the way for the return of Borodin and Galen to Hankow.

There were no sanctions, and Japan, having been formally condemned at Geneva for her action in Manchuria, withdrew from membership of the League of Nations, taking with her as a souvenir the Pacific islands held under League Mandate. Just before the Geneva verdict and Japan's notice of withdrawal Hitler became Chancellor of Germany, and his triumph was a guarantee that there would not be for some years to come any united front of the Western Powers to curb Japan's new forward policy in East Asia. Japanese statesmen, observing the tangle of European policies from the other side of the great Eurasian continent, noted with satisfaction the widening schism in the European order, the new stress and strain imposed on it by the emergence from Weimar pacifism of the grim Third Reich. Four Great Powers were among the nations sitting in judgement on Japan at Geneva and recording their unanimous opinion on her delinquency: four Great Powers, permanent members of the Council of the League—England, France, Italy, and Germany. But what a quartet to apply 'collective security'! What solidarity, what perfection of mutual trust, what disinterestedness of devotion to the reign of law, what capacity for harmonious co-operation! The four Great Powers and the fifty lesser states made indeed a brave array—at Geneva! But the Japanese admirals were not impressed.

Since the spring of 1933 Japan has played a lone hand in world politics, relying on her regional naval supremacy, her new competence in commercial competition, and the European preoccupations both of England and of Soviet Russia. It is above all the 'containing' of the two latter Powers by Nazi Germany which has been the condition of success for Japan in her new independence of policy. Even without the Anti-Comintern pact between Tokyo and Berlin, the Nazi régime serves the ambitions of Japan by its very existence, by the mere fact of German rearmament which compels all the states threatened by it to concentrate their strength in Europe. Germany, stripped of her colonies by the Versailles Treaty, is wholly within Europe; it is the ex-Allied Powers who must disperse their forces in order to secure their territories in Asia, where they are confronted no longer, as in the eighteenth and nineteenth centuries, by backward 'native' peoples, passively awaiting the European conqueror, but by a restlessly active warrior nation furnished with all the equipment necessary for twentieth-century *Machtpolitik*. England must look not only to the North Sea and the Low Countries, but also to Singapore; France not only to the Rhine, but also to Saigon; Russia not only to Kiev, but also to

Vladivostok. Measures have been taken to strengthen the defences of these outliers of European colonial expansion. England has now built at Singapore one of the most strongly fortified and fully equipped naval bases in the world and has virtually undertaken the defence, not only of her own colony of Malaya and the Dominion of Australia, but also of the Dutch East Indies and French Indo-China (since neither Holland nor France are able to provide adequately in present circumstances for the security of these possessions). In the northern sector of the Far East Soviet Russia has built up a strong system of defence for her territory, and at great expense has made provision for an independent Far Eastern Army with bombers and submarines at Vladivostok to harry Japan in case of a thrust into Siberia by the Japanese mainland forces. These preparations, to north and south of the central area of the Far East, are locally formidable deterrents to Japanese expansion. But the Powers sovereign at Singapore and Vladivostok are immobilized by the European tension; both of them wish to cut their Far Eastern risks and liabilities to a bare minimum in order to dispose of their utmost strength in Europe. England and Soviet Russia in the Far East are alike pinned down to the defence of their own territories, and neither is capable, in the present disposition of European politics, of a bold initiative to make history on the shores of the Pacific.[1]

[1] The situation would be entirely changed in the event of a renewal of the Russo-German entente which existed before 1933.

The Japanese Army, whose leaders have never quite reconciled themselves to the frustration of their Siberian empire-making design in 1918–22, has subjected the Soviet Far Eastern forces to several local trials of strength since it took over from China the Siberian frontiers of Manchuria. To weaken the Soviet power by cutting out the Russian sphere in North Manchuria was, indeed, an aim of the Army in its Manchurian campaign of 1931–3 second only to the primary purpose of settling scores with Chang Hsüeh-liang. It is even arguable that without this anti-Soviet objective Manchukuo would never have been created, for it would have been easy enough with a temporary Japanese occupation of the principal towns of South Manchuria to have dictated terms to Chang, just as the Russians had done by their invasion in 1929, and this would have been sufficient for the safeguarding of the threatened S.M.R. interests. But Blücher's successful border campaign had produced alarm as well as envy among the Japanese generals; it was clear that Soviet power in the Far East was increasing and would continue to grow with Russia's new industrialization. This power was hostile to Japan and threatened to reach out towards China through the Mongol Republic, which had been set up in 1924 by pro-Soviet Mon-

Such a reversal of Germany's present policy (which is known to be favoured by a section of the Reichswehr) would enable Russia to concentrate her strength in Asia, as during the period 1895–1905. So far, however, Hitler has preferred to base his foreign policy on the anti-Bolshevik crusade and the memories of Brest-Litovsk.

gols with the aid of the Russian Red Army. To the Japanese strategists the best way to cramp the Soviet power without an actual invasion of Russian territory seemed to be by a permanent occupation of North Manchuria, depriving the Russians of their C.E.R. short cut to Vladivostok. This was accomplished by the Japanese campaign, and the Soviet Far Eastern Army was not yet strong enough to challenge the procedure designed for its embarrassment. The Japanese refrained from any attempt to deprive the Soviet Union of its property rights in the C.E.R., but with Japanese troops in control of North Manchuria the railway no longer had value for Russia, and Moscow cut the loss by selling out (nominally to Manchukuo) in 1934. Even this victory did not satisfy a clique of Japanese Army extremists who wished to advance into Outer Mongolia and further outflank Russia's communications with the Far East by occupying Urga. But Russian resistance stiffened with the passing of time, and Admiral Okada, who was Prime Minister of Japan from 1934 to 1936, vetoed a fresh plunge into the Asiatic hinterland, fearing a diversion which would weaken Japan in her demand for revision of the Washington Naval Treaty.

There have been frequent alarms and rumours of an impending Russo-Japanese war, but even border 'incidents' involving artillery fire and aerial bombings have failed to bring about general hostilities. There has certainly been no lack of mutual exasperation, but war has not been to the interest of either party. The policy of the Soviet Union ever since Hitler's rise to power in Germany has been to conserve her strength for eventualities in Europe, while at the same time preparing to defend either Siberia or the Mongol Republic against Japanese invasion. Short of such invasion the policy requires that war in Asia be avoided. On the Japanese side the recklessness of certain army leaders has so far been restrained by more prudent counsels which the high command cannot ignore. Japan has already an excellent strategic position *vis-à-vis* Russia ; to seek further expansion to the north or north-west would involve the maximum of risk for the minimum of possible gain.

The pointer of Japanese expansion is towards China Proper and Inner Mongolia, not towards Outer Mongolia or Siberia. To west and south-west of Japan lie the lands over which the islanders seek to establish an ascendancy of power. The formulae of 'the stabilization of East Asia' and 'the Japan-Man-chukuo-China economic bloc' provide the watchwords for Tokyo's policy of making China, or at least the north-eastern provinces, into a domain of Japanese finance and commerce, with the Western Powers excluded or admitted only on terms. This Japanese penetration of China is the characteristic feature of the contemporary period of Far Eastern history dating from 1933. In the period of the Opening of the Gates both Japan and China were subjected to a semi-colonial domination by the invading Western

Powers; in the next stage Japan emancipated herself from the servitudes of the 'unequal treaties' while China fell more and more under the sway of Western imperialism; now, Japan has claimed the exploitation of China's weakness as a monopoly for herself and has given the Western Powers notice to quit.

There is a certain poetic justice in this discomfiture of the nations of the West by a people whom they have forcibly dragged from an innocuous self-seclusion and instructed in all the occult arts of their civilization from the practice of central banking to the handling of 16-inch guns. Japan has removed the stigma of inherent incapacity and futility which in the nineteenth century was attached to the adjective 'Asiatic'. Japan has claimed a place for Asia in that select ring of political arbiters of fate distinguished by the title of Great Powers. But it is only in a romantically generalized view of history that Japan can be regarded as the champion of Asia in its resurgence against the ascendancy of Europe. Actually Japan meets with the bitterest opposition from her fellow Asiatics and her pan-Asiatic propaganda has had little effect. The divisions of Europe are matched by those of Asia, and Japan is no more loved by the Chinese than is France by the Germans. The subject or partly dependent nationalities of Asia strive for independence and not a mere change of masters, even if such a change were not likely to aggravate their servitude. As it is, China fears the yoke of Japan more than that of any Western Power, not only because Japan is nearer and more capable of a direct domination, but also because her poverty in natural resources and her economic distresses make her heavy-handed in colonial management. These are considerations sufficient also to deter Filipinos, Annamese, and Malays from welcoming Japan as the deliverer of Asiatics from Western rule. But for China there is a still more powerful factor making for hostility to Japan. China declines to be Japan's satellite in a Far Eastern states system because of a deep-seated conviction that the rôle of leadership in Asia is one that belongs to herself, however incapable she may be at the moment of making her supremacy effective. The nationalism of the Kuomintang has altered the form of Chinese national pride, but not its spirit, and though China has humbled herself to the extent of going to school to learn what the West has to teach, she still finds it intolerable to be subject to direction by her own former pupil in civilization. Japan has stolen a march on China by adapting herself more rapidly to the conditions created by the Western invasion, and China cannot forgive her for it. Nor is this sentiment merely a product of outraged *amour propre*. The present-day preponderance of Japan in state power and her lead in economic development are, as it were, distortions of natural historical tendency, deformations of normal growth. There are five times as many Chinese as Japanese; the natural resources of China are immensely superior to those of Japan, and her great coalfields in Shensi, Shansi, and Hopei provinces make her much more suitable for large-scale industrialization. China is the main source of the traditional culture of Far Eastern lands and as late as the middle of the nineteenth century held a vast empire of subject and tributary peoples, including even the Japanese-speaking Ryukyu islanders, while Japanese power did not reach to the shore of the continent. So nearly did China fill the picture of the Far East in the popular imagination of Western countries in the 'seventies that the future Admiral Togo was nicknamed 'Johnny Chinaman' by the English midshipmen aboard the training ship *Worcester*, whither he was sent in 1872, and his protests that Japan was a distinct country were entirely disregarded. It was 'Johnny Chinaman' who thirty-three years later destroyed Russia's Baltic Fleet in the biggest naval battle between Trafalgar and Jutland—but it was not China's victory!

Chinese jealousy of Japan's achievement is matched by the Japanese fear of being overtaken by China now that the latter is at last fairly launched on the path of modernization. The Japanese are haunted by the vision of a new China, united, independent, and reorganized, steadily reducing her rival's temporary lead and finally surpassing her in wealth and power. This fear operates like the old German fear of 'encirclement' in reconciling the nation to a chauvinist programme. The Japanese seek to control China's development so that it may bring no injury to the vested interests of Japan economically or politically. If China were to make her own history in complete independence during the next two or three decades, it could hardly fail to be at Japan's expense, for the latter's industrial economy has been built up, in spite of Nature's disfavour, on the basis of a Japanese superiority in state power and technological accomplishment, and would be fatally deranged by a thorough industrialization of China carried out in the fashionable manner of economic nationalism. The 'Japan-Manchukuo-China economic bloc', which has become the slogan of Japanese imperialism, means that Japan is to plan and direct the economic life of this whole area and thus retain the ascendancy she gained by her march ahead in the Meiji era.

After the completion of the conquest of Manchuria there were many Japanese who hoped that it might be possible to stop at the Great Wall and gradually resume normal relations both with China and the Western Powers. But the new situation created by the conquest did not allow Japan to close the account. On the one hand, Manchukuo became an insuperable barrier to friendship and co-operation between Japan and China, an Alsace-Lorraine neither to be forgiven nor forgotten by the Chinese; on the other, Japan's economic and political development tended more and more to shape her policy in the direction of autarchy and territorial expansion.

A Chinese military reconquest of Manchuria was not immediately in the realm of practical politics, but Chinese resentment took the form of economic reprisals, including various tariff devices and discrimination against Japanese investment. The Japanese replied with 'special trade', a system of smuggling under armed guard through the demilitarized zone established by the Tangku Truce between China Proper and Manchukuo, but such methods merely aggravated the hostility of the Chinese and provoked further the resentment of Western nations whose commerce was damaged by them. By 1937 it was clear that China was not going to 'co-operate' in any of Japan's economic schemes, and that Japan must either abandon such schemes or promote them by force.

The main objective of the Army and of the heavy industrial interests was to acquire adequate supplies of good coking coal and high-grade iron ore within the currency area of the yen and under Japanese military control, so that they could not be cut off in time of war. Such supplies were not to be found in Japan Proper, Korea or Manchukuo,[1] but only in North China, notably in the provinces of Hopei, Chahar, and Shansi. Japan had already a military foothold in this region through the garrisons she was entitled, along with other foreign Powers, to keep stationed in Peiping and along the railway from Tientsin under the Boxer Protocol of 1901; moreover, she was able in 1935 to force the withdrawal of

---

[1] During 1938, however, large high-grade iron-ore deposits are said to have been discovered in the mountains of eastern Manchukuo near the Korean border.

ADMIRAL OKADA

Prime Minister of Japan, 1934–6

Chinese Central Government troops from Hopei. But the provincial troops remained hostile and Japan could obtain no facilities for mining enterprises. The Lung Yen iron works about twelve miles west of Peiping, constructed with Japanese capital under the pro-Japanese Anfu government in 1920 for smelting ores from Chahar, had never been opened and stood derelict until last year.

The question of currency affected cotton and other raw materials as well as coal and iron. Japan's currency weakness and dependence on large imports of raw materials both for her export trade manufactures and also for her increased armaments led to a drive for extending the 'yen bloc' so as to effect the maximum saving of gold and foreign exchange. A managed currency linked to the yen had been established in Manchukuo, and on November 4, 1935, it was announced that the Manchukuo yuan and the yen would henceforth be held at par. To quote an American writer on this financial system:[1]

'While exchange control has restricted payments to the outside world from either Japan or Manchukuo, it is now very easy to make payments between Japan and Manchukuo. . . . What the currency arrangement does is to allow trade with Manchukuo to be excluded from the increasingly stringent exchange controls which a weak yen has made necessary. By means of it Japan is able to make tremendous purchases in Manchukuo

[1] Warren S. Hunsberger, 'The Yen bloc in Japan's expansion program' in *Far Eastern Survey*, vii, no. 22, Nov. 9, 1938.

and carry on other activities such as investment, which the weakness of the yen would make impossible otherwise.'

The idea of extending the system to cover investments and purchases of raw materials in North China followed inevitably from its success in Manchukuo, and attempts were made by threats and intrigue to set up an 'autonomous' government of the 'Five Northern Provinces' (Hopei, Chahar, Suiyuan, Shansi, and Shantung) with a currency of its own. But these attempts failed, and China, with the advice of Sir Frederick Leith-Ross who was sent out for the purpose from England in the winter of 1935-6, carried out a thorough-going monetary reform which linked the Chinese currency with sterling and thus accentuated Japan's financial difficulties.

The strongest objection to Japanese Army plans for advancing into North China came from naval circles; the rival service believed that Japan ought to concentrate on sea-power and avoid the perilous lengthening of land frontiers which any military occupation in China Proper must involve. The Navy was able to exert a decisive influence on policy as long as Admiral Okada was Prime Minister—that is to say, down to February 1936. Its hold on the country, however, was largely due to the diversion of public attention from Asiatic affairs by the negotiations for renewal of the Washington Naval Treaty, and once these had reached and passed their climax, interest began to revert to the aims of continental policy. The military mutiny of February 26 over-threw the Okada Cabinet, though the mutineers were forced to surrender and the ringleaders were shot. The weakness of the Navy as a political force was mainly due to two factors: in the first place, as a service with a small professional personnel it could not compete with the conscript army in popular in-fluence, and secondly, the desire for assured supplies for the armaments industry prevailed among the admirals no less than among the generals, and the former could not show how they were to be obtained except by invading North China.

The war which is now in progress in the Far East began as a local campaign in Hopei in July 1937, but soon spread, as did the Manchurian fighting in 1932, to Shanghai, and the 'incident' became a straight war between Japan and China. Shanghai and Nanking having been lost, the 'Nanking Govern-ment' retreated to Hankow with the Canton–Hankow railway as its main line of communication with the outer world. The Japanese for a long time refrained from attacking Canton, partly because of the im-mobilization of large forces in Manchukuo by the menace of Blücher's Soviet Far Eastern Army and partly because of fear of complications with the British at Hong Kong. But after the occultation of Blücher and the unextended battle of Changkufêng in August 1938 had proved to their satisfaction that the Russians were in no mood for an offensive war, and after the Munich Agreement had fully revealed the contractionist tendency of British foreign policy, the Japanese took the bull by the horns, fitted out an expeditionary force and captured Canton nine days after a landing on the shores of Bias Bay. A threat to occupy Hainan was sufficient to induce the French to be careful about traffic on the Haiphong–Yunnan railway, and the separation of independent China from the neutral shipping of the China Seas was thus rendered virtually complete. China was now shut up in her unindustrialized hinterland and brought to depend, for communication with the outer world, on two brave, but insufficient, new roads—the desert road to the Soviet Union *via* Hami and Urumchi and the mountain road to Burma *via* Yunnan and Kunming.

Since Canton and Hankow fell to the Japanese the struggle has entered on a phase in which military skill and armaments are of less importance than patience and resolution. From a purely strategic point of view the position appears to be one of stalemate; it seems equally improbable either that the Japanese can subdue the Kuomintang forces in the mountain-girt provinces of Western China or that the latter can recapture unaided any of the key cities now held by the Japanese. The conflict thus becomes one of political and economic attrition. Each side holds strong cards and each declares its willingness for hostilities of indefinite duration. The Japanese control all the maritime outlets of China and their warships possess the Yangtse up to Yochow—a 10,000-ton cruiser can go to Hankow when the river is at its height; they hold six out of what were two years ago the seven largest cities of China; they are sustained morally by their formidable partners in the Anti-Comintern Pact. The Chinese, on the other hand, have more than half of their country still un-invaded and most of the rest of it controlled by their guerrilla bands behind the Japanese lines; their armies after terrible mauling show an undefeated spirit; their currency is supported by the pound and the dollar, and credits are now forthcoming from British and American sources for roads and lorries. Each side likewise has suffered great disappointments; the Japanese have been unpleasantly surprised by the resistance of the Chinese and the duration of the war, whereas the Chinese have been grievously disillu-sioned in their expectations of foreign intervention in their favour.

To-day[1] China could probably obtain peace by comparatively small concessions to Japan and might even with Japanese aid obtain some compensation for her losses at the expense of third parties. It is just possible that this may still happen; we have seen how in Europe the deserted Czechs have made their terms with the Nazi Reich. But the Japanese have provoked a hatred in China which it will be hard indeed for them to live down. General Ugaki, while Foreign Minister of Japan, declared that it was his intention to make it up with China after the war as Bismarck had made it up with Austria after Sadowa. Bismarck,

[1] January 1939.

however, was only able to do this because he spared Austria's pride and deliberately refrained from the triumphal entry into Vienna which he might have had. The Japanese have shown little capacity for sugaring the bitterness of defeat; their widespread pillaging and wrecking of China's infant industries have alienated just those classes in China which might have been expected, from their dislike of Communism and desire for a quiet life, to have favoured peace with Japan at almost any price. If the invaders despoil the supple-policied compradores and landlord-merchants who might make over a reasonable portion of China's resources to a discreet coercion, who is there to play off against that innumerable multitude of the poor whom the Communists draw after them? It is true that the Communists are not what they were; now that the Comintern has subordinated the international struggle of the proletariat to the bargains of the Soviet Union with particular capitalist states, they have transformed themselves into anti-Japanese ultra-nationalists with a domestic programme of mild social reform. But red or pink, their name is a legend for the masses in China and they cannot be bought or intimidated by Japan. With Shanghai in ruins and the Eighth Route Army forever marching by night in Shansi, it is not easy to see how the Japanese are going to give political substance to a Japan-Manchukuo-China economic bloc.

Japan may succeed in consolidating her hold on

the coal and iron resources of Hopei and Inner Mongolia and creating that heavy industry base which is her principal economic objective. But there is no end in sight to her feud with China, and meanwhile a new threat to her power is emerging on the other side of the Pacific. The U.S.A. is again, as in 1918, beginning to arm herself on a scale commensurate with her latent strength. The new American navy programme provides for ships of an unprecedented cruising radius and is plainly designed to enable the United States to fight a war in the *western* Pacific. Already Senator Pittman, Chairman of the Senate Foreign Relations Committee, has declared to the world that 'the American people does not like the government of Japan'. America has protested very sharply against the closing of the commercial Open Door in China, and pressure from the State Department has stopped the supply of aircraft to Japan from American firms. It may not be easy to drag the American people out of isolationism merely to give expression to a moral disapproval, but the U.S.A. is involved in Far Eastern affairs by the ultimately compelling logic of territorial possession. The Philippines are indeed supposed to become entirely independent in 1945, but that is six years away and there are reservations in the Act by which the Americans will be able to stay in the islands until the Greek Kalends if they so desire. What is more, there is no longer, now the Washington Naval Treaty has lapsed, anything to prevent them from making a battle-fleet base out of the present cruiser base at Cavite near Manila. Nothing would alter the present balance of forces in the Far East so much as this. The power of America is not, like that of England or Russia, immobilized by the tensions of Europe; it can be directed either eastwards or westwards according to policy, and it can hardly be doubted that in the near future the U.S.A. will be the foremost of the Western Powers in the Far East, the residuary legatee of the Portuguese, Dutch, and British maritime hegemonies of earlier days. It is by negotiation between Tokyo and Washington—or by ordeal of battle in the China Seas—that the great issues of Far Eastern politics are likely in the next decade to be decided.

INDEX

Aleutian Is., 201.

Alliances:
    Anglo-French, of 1854–60, 22, 56–8, 67.
    Anglo-Japanese, 122–7, 135; renewals of, 143, 184; end of, 202.
    Franco-Russian, 75–7, 88, 94, 96, 108, 135–9, 151, 167.
    Russo-Chinese, 93, 98, 100.
    Triple, 76, 138–40.

Amherst, Embassy of Lord, 16, note.

Amoy, 17.

Amur, 55–9, 61, 71, 156, 158.

Anfu, Chinese party, 208, 212, 217.

Annam, 23, 65–8.

Arthur, Port, 86–90, 99–102, 117, 120, 129, 132–3, 145, 151.

Austria, 74–6, 138.

Baikal, Lake, 56, 71, 189, 190.

Balfour, Mr., 105.

Balkans, Russian policy and the, 74, 76, 138.

Behaine, Pigneau de, Bishop of Adran, 66.

Belgium, concession for Peking-Hankow railway to, 106.

Bengkulen, 5, 9, 10.

Bjorkö, Treaty of, 137.

Blücher, Marshal (*see also* Galen), 261.

Bonin Is., 201.

Borneo, 10–11.

Borodin, 214, 216, 223, 224.

Boxers, the, 117–19, 203.

Boycotts, Chinese, 194, 242, 244, 245.

Britain, policy of, 4–7, 9–11, 16–18, 22, 51–5, 73–4, 84, 88–90, 102–10, 113–16, 119–22, 125–7, 135, 143–4, 155, 174, 182–6, 222–5.

Brunei, 11.

Bülow, Count von, 121, 127.

Burma, 68.

Cambodia, 7, 66, 67.

Canning, 6.

Canton, 12, 14–17, 22, 51–2, 168, 178, 205, 211–12, 218, 223, 226.

Caroline Is., 174.

Cassini, Count, 98.

Castlereagh, 5.

Celebes, 10.

Chamberlain, Sir Austen, 224.

Chamberlain, Joseph, 116, 120.

Chams, the, 65.

Chang Hsüeh-liang, 232–3, 237–40, 247, 261.

Chang Tso-lin, 206, 208–11, 219, 226, 229–32.

Changchun, 145, 152.

Chapdelaine, 22.

Chekiang, 33, 217.

Ch'en Ch'iung-ming, 212.

Chiang Kai-shek, 217–23, 225, 232, 235, 239.

Ch'ien Lung, Emperor, 13, 16, note.

Chihli (Hopei), 79, 160; Chinese faction, 208, 210, 217.

Chinchow-Aigun railway scheme, 156–7.

Chinese Eastern Railway, 92–4, 151, 154, 208–10, 228–9, 236–8, 262.

Choshu, 26, 42, 43, 45–6.

Christian missions, 22, 33–6.

Comintern, the, 214, 216.

Communism, Chinese, 216, 220, 222–3, 225–6.

Index

Confucianism, 28–31, 33–6, 48, 207.
Consortium, Bankers', for loans to China, 167, 169, 171.
Crimean War, the, 22, 57.
Customs, Chinese Imperial Maritime, 23, 166.
Czechoslovak Legionaries, the, 186–8.

Daimyo, 36–7.
Defence Force, the British Shanghai, 222, 223.
Delcassé, 135.
Deutsch-Asiatische Bank, the, 97.
Devonshire, Duke of, speech by, 113.
Diedrichs, Admiral, 109.
Dogger Bank Incident, the, 136.
Dragomirov, General, 74.
Dreibund, the East Asiatic, 77, 88, 89, 97, 99, 104, 110, 136.
Dufferin, Lord, Viceroy of India, 69.

East India Company, the English, 7, 9, 12, 14, 16.
Eckhardstein, 122.
England, *see* Britain.
Ententes :
　Anglo-French, 108, 135, 143, 151.
　Anglo-Russian, 150–1.
　Franco-Japanese, 149.
　Russo-Japanese, 145, 149, 157, 159, 185.
Extraterritoriality, 18, 19, 22, 82, 83, 227, 234, 235.

Fakumen railway concession, the, 155.
Fashoda Incident, the, 107–8.
Feng Yu-hsiang, 219, 225, 226, 239.
Fengtien, Chinese party, 208, 219.

Foochow, 17.
Formosa, 86.
France, policy of, 3, 4, 22, 65–70, 75–7, 87, 92, 94–8, 102, 107, 135, 150, 167, 178, 188–90, 201.
French Concession, Shanghai, the, 20.
Fukien, 53, 131, 168.

Galen (*see also* Blücher), 216, 223.
Germany, policy of, 75–7, 87, 96–100, 109, 114, 121–2, 126, 135–9, 143, 258–9.
Gobi desert, the, 73, 161, 164.
Graves, General, 190.
Guam, 201, 270.
Guards, railway, 94, 145, 228.

Hainan, 98.
Hamaguchi, 245.
Hamilton, Port, 84.
Hankow, 106, 219, 222–5.
Harbin, 102.
Harding, President, 198.
Harriman, 153, 156.
Hastings, Lord, 6.
Hatzfeldt, Count, 121.
Hawaii, 201, 250, 252.
Hay, Secretary, 111.
Hayashi, Count, 123, 125, 130.
Heitoukai, battle of, 142.
Hicks Beach, Sir M., speech by, 103.
Hirota, Mr., 269.
Holland, policy of, 5, 8–11, 24.
Hong Kong, 17, 51–4, 63, 68, 95, 104, 228.
Hong merchants, the, 17.
Hopei (*see also* Chihli), 265.
Hoppo, the, Chinese official, 15.
Hung Hsiu-ch'üan, 34.

Indemnity Loans to China, the, 92, 97.
India, 4, 9, 15, 67, 69, 73, 143–4.
Indo-China, French, 68, 95, 102, 260.

Index

Inouye, Meiji statesman, 42; Finance Minister in 1929–31, 243.

International Settlement, Shanghai, the, 20, 222, 235.

Intervention, the Triple, 1895, 87–90.

— anti-Bolshevik, in Siberia, 1918–20, 186–191.

Irkutsk, 71.

Isolation, British, 107, 119; American, 120.

Ito, Marquis, 42, 123–5.

Java, 4, 5, 10.

Johore, 6.

Kagoshima, 26, 41.

Kaiser, see William II.

Kalmikov, Ataman, 190.

Kamchatka, 56, 59.

K'ang Yu-wei, 118.

Kato, Admiral, 245.

Katsura, Prince, 124, 153.

Kellogg Pact, the, 238.

Kenseikai, Japanese party, 193.

Khabarovsk, 71.

Khilkov, Prince, 134.

Khutukhtu, the, 164.

Kiakhta, 56.

Kianghwa, Treaty of, 83.

Kiaochow, 98–102, 173, 178, 196.

Kirin, 62, 127.

Knox, Secretary, 156.

Kojiki, the, 44.

Kolchak, Admiral, 189–90.

Komura, Baron, 154.

Korea, 59, 74, 78, 80–6, 94, 123, 125, 131–2, 144–5, 157, 249.

Kowloon, 53.

Kuge, 36, 37.

Kuo Sun-ling, 229.

Kuomintang, the, 169–71, 177, 211–36, 239.

Kurile Is., 59–61, 201.

Kuropatkin Line, the, 161.

Kwangchow-wan, 102, 104, 228.

Kwangsi, 22, 52, 95, 102, 150, 212.

Kwangtung, 52, 98, 102, 168, 212.

Kwantung Leased Territory, the, 175, 228; Army, 267.

Lampson, Sir Miles, 224.

Lanchow, 160.

Lansdowne, Lord, 125, 135.

Laos, province of French Indo-China, 68.

Lascelles, Sir Frank, 141.

Lazarev, Port, 84.

League of Nations, 179, 181, 252–6.

Leased Territories in China, 99–104, 228.

Li Hung-chang, 79, 93, 100.

Li Lien-ying, 79.

Liao river, the, 85, 128.

Liaotung, 86–7.

Lin Tse-hsü, 14, 17.

Loans to China, 92, 97, 165–7, 169–71, 177, 240.

Lu Yung-hsiang, 217.

Lyons, Chamber of Commerce of, trade mission to China, 95.

Macao, 17.

Macartney, Embassy of Lord, 13, 16, note.

Malacca, 4–6, 8–10.

Manchukuo, 147, 211, 232, 247, 261, 262.

Manchuria, 61–3, 85, 91–4, 105, 116, 119, 122–3, 127, 132, 145–9, 152–9, 175, 207–11, 227–33, 237–40, 249, 254, 262.

Manchus, the, 31, 47, 55–6, 62, 162, 163.

Manila, 109, 201.

Marianne Is., 174.

Marshall Is., 174.

Meiji, Emperor, 47.

Minami, General, 246.

Minseito, Japanese party, 193, 242–7.

Index

Möllendorff, von, 84.
Moluccas, the, 9. [262.
Mongolia, 56, 159–65, 175, 249,
Morocco, 135, 137, 140.
Most-favoured-nation treatment,
  17–18, 82, 86, 227.
Motono-Isvolsky Agreement, the,
  149.
Mukden, province, 128; battle
  of, 134; Incident of 1931, 247.
Muraviev-Amurski, 60.
Muraviev, Count, Russian For-
  eign Minister, 99, 115.

Nagasaki, 24, 25.
Nanking, 219, 221; Govern-
  ment, 222, 225, 227, 231, 233,
  235; Treaty of, 17–21, 33.
Napier, Lord, 16–17, 51.
Napoleon III, 22, 66.
Nicholas II, Tsar, 93, 100, 121,
  135–8.
Nikolaievsk Massacre, the, 191.
Ningpo, 17.
Nishihara, Mr., 177.
Novosti, the, 128.

Okada, Admiral, 262, 270.
Okhotsk Sea, 50, 55, 56.
Open Door policy, the, 55, 102,
  105, 110–15, 155, 190, 200.
Opium, 14.

Palmerston, 17.
Peking, 22, 23, 57, 116, 118, 141,
  249; Government, the, 177,
  205–11, 217, 219, 227.
Peking–Hankow railway conces-
  sion, the, 106.
Pelew Is., 174.
Penang, 5.
Perry, Commodore, 25.
Pescadores Is., 68, 86.
Petropavlovsk, 57.
Philippines, the, 11, 109, 201.

Portsmouth, Treaty of, 144–7,
  249.

Portuguese, the, 2, 8, 9, 11, 205.
Possadnik, the, 63.
Primorsk, the, 62–3.

Racial Equality, demand for
  recognition of, 181–2.
Raffles, Sir Stamford, 4–7, 10.
Railways, in China, Concessions
  for, 93, 102, 105–6, 114, 155–7.
Reorganization Loan, the, 169.
Revolution, the Chinese, 162,
  168.
Ronin, 42, 268.
Russia, policy of, 55–65, 71–8,
  84, 86–7, 90–4, 98–102, 115–
  17, 119, 124, 128, 132, 137–
  43, 158–65, 167, 208–11, 229,
  238, 248, 249, 262.
Russo-Chinese Bank, the, 92,
  106.
Russo-Korean Bank, the, 94.

Saionji, Prince, 148.
Sakhalin, 59–61, 145, 191.
Salt Gabelle, the, 171.
Samurai, 37–42, 46.
Sarawak, 11.
Sazonov, 158.
Seiyukai, Japanese party, 193,
  230, 242, 244, 247.
Semenov, Ataman, 190.
Shanghai, 17, 20, 23, 89, 219,
  222, 223, 235.
Shanhaikwan, 231, 247.
Shansi, 226, 231, 265.
Shantung, 98, 102–4, 114, 118,
  174–5, 178–81, 194–6, 230,
  244.
Shidehara, Baron, 243, 246.
Shimonoseki, 26, 41, 42.
Shogunate, the, 25, 26, 38, 41,
  44–6.
Siam, 7, 69.
Singapore, 4, 6, 7, 10, 201,
  251, 260.
Socony Hill, Nanking, 221.

Index

South Manchuria Railway, the, 154, 175, 228, 230, 236, 240, 242, 245.
Soviet Union, *see* Russia.
Spanish-American War, the, 109.
Spee, Admiral von, 173.
Spheres of influence, 104-6, 111-14, 116, 149-50, 159.
Sun Chuan-fang, 219.
Sun Yat-sen, 170, 171, 205, 211, 212, 214, 217.
Szechwan, 95, 168.

T'ai P'ing rebellion, the, 23, 34-5, 48-9, 57.
Takarabe, Admiral, 245.
Talienwan, 99.
Tanaka, General Baron, 230, 244.
Tao Kuang, Emperor, 32.
Tariff, restriction of Chinese, 17, 21, 23, 166; Smoot-Hawley, 242.
Terauchi, General Count, 177.
Thibaw, King of Burma, 68.
Tientsin, 118.
Times, The, 89, 90, 134.
Timor, 11.
Togo, Admiral, 134, 250, 266.
Tonghaks, the, 85.
Tongking, 65-8, 95.
Tozama clans, the, 38.
Trans-Caspian Railway, the, 72.
Trans-Siberian Railway, the, 71-2, 75, 91-3, 187.
Trotsky, 187.
Tsinan, 196, 231.
Tsingtao, 173, 196.
Tsushima, 63, 134.
Tuan Chi-jui, 177, 208.
T'ungmenghui, 211.
Twenty-one Demands, the, 175.
Tze-hsi, Empress, 118, 170.

United States of America, policy of, 24, 110, 115, 146, 156, 171, 179-82, 190, 196-9, 249-51, 269-71, 275-6.
Urga, 164, 261.
Urup, 60.
Ussuri, 59, 63.

Venezuela-Guiana boundary dispute, the, 109.
Versailles Treaty, the, 179, 194-6.
Vladivostok, 62, 63, 71, 187, 188, 260, 262.

Wakatsuki, Baron, 246, 247.
Waldersee, Count von, 119.
Wanpaoshan, 242, 245.
Washington Conference and Treaties, the, 199-202, 248, 250.
Weihaiwei, 103-4, 228, note.
'West China', 160.
Whampoa military academy, the, 217.
Whangpoo river, the, 20.
William II, German Emperor, 88, 100, 121, 135-8, 141, 249.
Wilson, President, 179-82.
Witte, Count, 86, 137, 138, 155, 160.
Wu P'ei-fu, 206, 208, 219.

Yalu, the, 132.
Yamagata, Marshal, 131.
Yang Yu-ting, General, 232, 233.
Yangtse, the, 20, 95, 105, 141, 168, 218, 219, 221.
Yedo, 25, 38, 41, 43, 45.
Yeh Ting, General, 226.
Yen Hsi-shan, General, 226, 239.
Yezo, 59, 60.
Yoshinobu, 46.
Yuan Shih-k'ai, 83, 170-2, 175-7.
Yunnan, 95, 102, 150, 212, 218.